Federal Acquisition Regulation (FAR) in Plain English

700+ Answers to Frequently Asked Questions (FAQ) about the FAR and Government Contracts

Christoph Mlinarchik
www.ChristophLLC.com
Christoph@ChristophLLC.com

About the Author, Christoph Mlinarchik

Christoph LLC provides expert advice in government contracts: consulting, expert witness services, and professional training. Contact Christoph LLC for solutions or to receive free, monthly updates on government contracts: **Christoph@ChristophLLC.com**

Owner Christoph Mlinarchik, JD, CFCM, PMP (Certified Federal Contract Manager, Project Management Professional) is an attorney, expert witness, professional instructor, consultant, frequent public speaker, nationally recognized subject matter expert, and award-winning author of 75+ publications on government contracts and acquisitions, including the books Government Contracts in Plain English (available at **https://www.amazon.com/dp/173419815X/**) and Federal Acquisition Regulation (FAR) in Plain English and Government Contracts Negotiation, Simplified! (available at **https://www.amazon.com/dp/1734198133**). Christoph was honored with the "Top Professionals Under 40" and "Best Article" awards by the National Contract Management Association (NCMA). Christoph Mlinarchik is an experienced expert witness who has delivered expert opinions and reports, research concerning damages, key findings, and case strategy for complex contracts litigation.

Christoph's consulting clients include businesses within information technology (IT), professional services, defense, cybersecurity, construction, medical/health care, intelligence, national security, research, science/technology, and several other sectors. Online courses are available at **Courses.ChristophLLC.com**. Christoph has taught or trained 1000+ federal, military, and contractor professionals nationwide—from novices to C-level executives. Contracts managers, attorneys, chief executive officers, program managers, sales directors, business capture and proposal experts, and other contracting professionals consistently provide outstanding reviews for Christoph's consulting expertise, teaching skills, presentation style, and client satisfaction.

Christoph has negotiated, reviewed, or managed billions of dollars of government contracts over the course of his career. This real-world experience provides an invaluable perspective for clients.

Copyright © 2021
Christoph Mlinarchik
www.ChristophLLC.com
Christoph@ChristophLLC.com
All rights reserved.
ISBN: 978-1-7341981-1-9

Table of Contents

Introductory Chapter 1, Federal Acquisition Regulation (FAR) in Plain English 1

Introductory Chapter 2, No, the FAR Does Not Apply to Government Contractors 9

Introductory Chapter 3, The Christian Doctrine and Missing Government Contract Clauses 11

Introductory Chapter 4, How to Research FAR Clauses 15

FAR Part 1, Federal Acquisition Regulations System 19

FAR Part 2, Definitions of Words and Terms 31

FAR Part 3, Improper Business Practices and Personal Conflicts of Interest 33

FAR Part 4, Administrative and Information Matters 41

FAR Part 5, Publicizing Contract Actions 47

FAR Part 6, Competition Requirements 51

FAR Part 7, Acquisition Planning 57

FAR Part 8, Required Sources of Supplies and Services 63

FAR Part 9, Contractor Qualifications 71

FAR Part 10, Market Research 75

FAR Part 11, Describing Agency Needs 79

FAR Part 12, Acquisition of Commercial Items 85

FAR Part 13, Simplified Acquisition Procedures 91

Table of Contents, Continued

FAR Part 14, Sealed Bidding 99

FAR Part 15, Contracting By Negotiation 103

FAR Part 16, Types of Contracts 127

FAR Part 17, Special Contracting Methods .143

FAR Part 18, Emergency Acquisitions 149

FAR Part 19, Small Business Programs 151

FAR Part 20, Reserved 161

FAR Part 21, Reserved 163

FAR Part 22, Application of Labor Laws to Government Acquisitions 165

FAR Part 23, Environment, Energy and Water Efficiency, Renewable Energy Technologies, Occupational Safety, and Drug-Free Workplace 169

FAR Part 24, Protection of Privacy and Freedom of Information . 171

FAR Part 25, Foreign Acquisition 173

FAR Part 26, Other Socioeconomic Programs 175

FAR Part 27, Patents, Data, and Copyrights .177

FAR Part 28, Bonds and Insurance 179

FAR Part 29, Taxes 185

FAR Part 30, Cost Accounting Standards Administration 187

Table of Contents, Continued

FAR Part 31, Contract Cost Principles and Procedures 191

FAR Part 32, Contract Financing 193

FAR Part 33, Protests, Disputes, and Appeals 197

FAR Part 34, Major System Acquisition 209

FAR Part 35, Research and Development Contracting 211

FAR Part 36, Construction and Architect-Engineer Contracts ... 217

FAR Part 37, Service Contracting 219

FAR Part 38, Federal Supply Schedule Contracting 223

FAR Part 39, Acquisition of Information Technology 225

FAR Part 40, Reserved 229

FAR Part 41, Acquisition of Utility Services 231

FAR Part 42, Contract Administration and Audit Services 233

FAR Part 43, Contract Modifications 235

FAR Part 44, Subcontracting Policies and Procedures 241

FAR Part 45, Government Property 251

FAR Part 46, Quality Assurance 253

FAR Part 47, Transportation 257

FAR Part 48, Value Engineering 259

FAR Part 49, Termination of Contracts 261

Table of Contents, Continued

FAR Part 50, Extraordinary Contractual Actions and the SAFETY Act 267

FAR Part 51, Use of Government Sources by Contractors 269

FAR Part 52, Solicitation Provisions and Contract Clauses 271

FAR Part 53, Forms 283

Conclusion: Are You a Professional? 285

Introductory Chapter 1, Federal Acquisition Regulation (FAR) in Plain English

Government contracting can be complex and difficult, but this book makes it simple and easy for you.

Before I answer 700+ of *your* frequently asked questions (FAQs) about the Federal Acquisition Regulation (FAR), let's start with two questions from me to you: Have you read the entire FAR? Do you *want* to read the entire FAR—from start to finish?

Probably not, but I have great news. I read it for you all the way through! I read the entire FAR, several times. I wrote a book that summarizes the "highlight reel" and you made a wise decision by purchasing it. By reading this book, you gain the insights I developed from years of experience in a variety of government contracting positions as a federal contract specialist, Judge Advocate General acquisitions attorney, professor, consultant to major corporations, small business advisor, published author, and expert witness in multi-million-dollar litigation.

I started my company **www.ChristophLLC.com** years ago to offer expert advice on government contracting. My company delivers consulting advice to federal contractors and subcontractors, professional training, and expert witness services. Pat yourself on the back; you just saved yourself hundreds of hours. Feel free to send me an email: **Christoph@ChristophLLC.com**. Complete my online courses at **Courses.ChristophLLC.com**.

What is the FAR?

The FAR or Federal Acquisition Regulation is the "Bible" of government contracting. It is the most important set of regulations that you must consult and study.

You will probably read snippets of the FAR in your government contract. The FAR specifies standard clauses to insert into government contracts. Always remember that the FAR provides instructions and directions chiefly to federal employees, specifically, to contracting officers. The FAR, however, does not apply to federal contractors although some clauses, sections, or snippets of the FAR may still apply to your company—if you find it in your contract. Please read Introductory Chapter 2, "No, the FAR Does Not Apply to Government Contractors."

Why doesn't this book list specific dollar thresholds from the FAR?

The FAR changes constantly. For this reason, I have chosen not to include specific dollar thresholds so that my summaries and short answers remain "evergreen" (permanently useful). I am saving you the expense of buying new updates of my book!

Why is this book written in plain English?

This book is written in plain English so you can quickly grasp the important concepts found within the FAR. Think of my book as the "highlight reel" of the FAR.

Does this book translate into plain English every single line of the FAR?

No, my book does not translate into plain English every single line of the FAR. Doing so would make my book unwieldy and impractical.

I carefully selected the "highlight reel" of the FAR to condense thousands of pages of regulations. This book delivers useful information from an experienced insider, but it cannot cover every topic or circumstance in the FAR. If you need help with a specific problem in government contracting, email me at **Christoph@ChristophLLC.com**. You can also learn more by taking my online courses at **Courses.ChristophLLC.com**.

How is this book organized?

Other than the introductory chapters and conclusion, this book includes chapters for all 53 parts of the FAR. Each chapter title matches the corresponding title in the FAR. For example, FAR Part 10 of this book is "Market Research" because FAR Part 10 is titled "Market Research."

Is this book an expert witness report with precise and cautious statements?

No, this book is not an expert witness report.

Is this book a series of short, practical answers for the busy professional?

Yes! This book gives you the basics — in plain English — of the most important set of regulations in government contracting, the Federal Acquisition Regulation (FAR). My book simplifies many complex ideas into sound bites — short, practical answers.

What is one reason clients hire Christoph LLC?

My clients love how I explain complicated things in a simple way. In fact, my streamlining is the primary reason why they hire me. They need an expert who can discover the important issues quickly and deliver plans of action that solve their problems. Don't you want someone to make it simple for you? I use as little jargon or confusing words as possible with my clients. I provide details when appropriate, but I always give the *bottom line up front* or *BLUF*. Whether I'm teaching a class of 50 students or advising the CEO of a corporation, I provide real world, practical advice.

Will this book provide instructions to federal contracting officers on how to perform their job in every situation?

No! My book is not a handbook to explain exactly what the government contracting officer must do in every situation. Instead, this book delivers a simplification of the major themes within each section of the FAR. I think my book is useful to both government contractors and federal employees, like contracting officers, contracting officer's representatives, and program managers. However, it is not a complete manual for how to do your job.

Is this book legal advice? Is this book tax advice? Is this book accounting advice?

No, no, and no! This book is not legal advice, which should come from a licensed attorney. My book is not tax advice, which should come from a competent tax professional. This book is not accounting advice, which should come from a certified public accountant (CPA). My book is a practical overview in plain English of the most important topics in the Federal Acquisition Regulation—the "highlight reel."

If you have a specific problem, you need a specific answer from a competent professional. My email address is **Christoph@ChristophLLC.com.**

Why is this book written in question-and-answer format?

The question-and-answer format is familiar to anyone who has read a frequently asked questions (FAQ) document. By writing my book in a question-and-answer format, you feel like we're having a conversation as you read. Finally, reading questions and answers trains your mind to ask the right questions, and accelerates the pace of your reading.

Have you written any other books in plain English?

Yes! Check out all three books in *The Government Contracts in Plain English Series*, available in paperback and Kindle on Amazon: **https://www.amazon.com/dp/B09MRCMWBD?binding=paperback**. Government Contracts in Plain English and Government Contracts Negotiation, Simplified! are the first and third books.

Who are the important players representing my government client?

Most government contracts will involve a contracting officer, a contracting officer's representative (COR), and a program manager. You need to understand the titles and responsibilities of your government clients.

Who is the contracting officer?

Contracting officers have the authority to sign, administer, and terminate contracts on behalf of the federal government. They also have the authority to make such determinations as whether a product is specifically considered "commercial" or whether to exercise the next option year period of the contract.

What is a contracting officer's warrant?

The contracting officer's authority is specified by a *warrant*, which is a document defining the dollar value and types of government contracts the contracting officer has the authority to sign. For example, one contracting officer may have a warrant to sign contracts up to $10 million. Another may have a $500 million warrant. An unlimited warrant generally bears no dollar limit. Some warrants are limited to government contracts rather than grants, and others allow for the signature of any type of government acquisition or assistance agreement, including procurement contracts, grants, cooperative agreements, and "Other Transactions."

The warrant's dollar value limitation applies to the individual contract action, not to the underlying total contract value. For example, a contracting officer with a $10 million warrant can sign a $9 million modification to a $500 million contract. However, that same contracting officer cannot sign a new contract for $500 million.

You should know the specific limitations set by the warrants of each contracting officer you encounter. Respectfully request a copy of these warrants from each contracting officer you deal with. You can also ask the chief of the contracting office for a list of all the warrants or copies of the warrants.

Can any person other than the contracting officer make valid changes to my government contract?

No! Any changes or additions to your contract must go through the contracting officer. Be skeptical about any promises made or any assurances offered by any federal employee other than the contracting officer. Remember this adage: "Nothing is real until it comes from the contracting officer."

Your goal is to have a positive and professional relationship with the contracting officer, who holds a great deal of power over your future. When you need that modification in 10 days or fewer, you should hope that the contracting officer knows your name. Five minutes of your time in a phone call may save you or cost you millions of dollars later. Every phone call or in-person meeting is worth hundreds of emails. Be always friendly and respectful.

Who is the contracting officer's representative or COR?

Contracting officers stay busy. They may sign hundreds or thousands of contracts over their careers. Contracting officers cannot possibly administer every detail of every contract. Therefore, they delegate some of the administration to federal employees called *contracting officer's representatives* or *CORs*.

CORs are appointed by contracting officers, in writing, using a letter of designation. This letter will describe the specific COR duties and responsibilities, identify any limitations, and specify the applicable period and extent of the COR's authority to act on behalf of the contracting officer. If you frequently work with a COR, you should request a copy of the designation letter of that COR, written by the contracting officer.

Who is the program manager?

Program managers have authority over the entire portfolio, project, or program your contract may support. Program managers do not have contractual authority, but they do have power over the direction and continuation of the program. You need to keep the program manager happy. You must remember that when the program manager gives you some direction that changes your contractual rights, you must notify the contracting officer to make official changes in writing to your contract.

Who is more important — the contracting officer or the program manager?

It depends. Sometimes the contracting officer is more powerful and can ruin your relationship with the client. Sometimes the program manager really calls the shots, and the contracting officer is treated like an administrative clerk. You need to investigate your clients, get to know them, tread lightly, and determine how to navigate across conflicting priorities. Information, insights, or opinions about these dynamics are invaluable.

Can I hire you for consulting, training, or expert witness services?

Maybe. Email me at **Christoph@ChristophLLC.com**. You can read more about my background and company at **www.ChristophLLC.com**. My online courses are available at **Courses.ChristophLLC.com**.

Introductory Chapter 2, No, the FAR Does Not Apply to Government Contractors

Is the door closed? I'm going to share one of the biggest secrets in government contracting. Everyone in the government contracts world has heard of the Federal Acquisition Regulation or FAR. Some call it the "Bible" for government contracts. Are you sitting down? Take a deep breath, because I have some shocking news for you: *The FAR does not apply to government contractors!* I wrote a full-length article on this topic, and I'm happy to send it to you if you email **Christoph@ChristophLLC.com**. But here's the crisp summary for the busy executive.

Does the FAR apply to government contractors?

No, the FAR applies to the federal employees involved in acquisition, namely, the contracting officers. Think of the FAR as the book of instructions to contracting officers as to which FAR clauses to include in the contract. If you want proof, read FAR 1.104, which explains that the FAR applies to all acquisitions. "Acquisition," according to FAR 2.101, means "the acquiring by contract... by and for the use of the Federal Government." Case closed. The FAR applies to acquisitions conducted by the federal government. Therefore, the FAR applies only to federal employees, not to federal contractors.

Is the FAR important for federal contractors to understand?

Yes, the FAR is extremely important to federal contractors, but only insofar as their contracts include certain FAR clauses. These FAR clauses are the connecting tissue between the government and the contractor. As such, individual FAR clauses must be included in the contract, or else they are not relevant (saving complicating factors like the Christian doctrine for another time). For more info, read Introductory Chapter 3, "The Christian Doctrine and Missing Government Contract Clauses."

Is the entire FAR incorporated into my government contract?

No, the entire FAR is not incorporated into your federal contract. That's not how things work. Instead, individual clauses are included on a case-by-case basis.

What should I do if someone sends me a FAR citation not found in my contract?

Do not fall for the bluff of a FAR citation that is not in your contract! Both the government and your private sector business partners will try to fool you, but do not fall for this common trick. You are reading my book. You know better! Follow your contract.

Why should I care if a FAR citation is found within my contract?

When you get a FAR citation, check immediately to see if that clause is in your contract. If it is not in your contract, why should you care about it? Is there a portion of your contract that incorporates that section of the FAR? If not, your opponent is blowing smoke.

Government contracting officers are famous for attempting this trick. They hit you with a FAR citation and say "The FAR requires that you do this. Please comply." Now you know how to handle this ruse. Ask for the page number of your contract that requires you to comply. Be respectful and polite but stand your ground.

Should I follow my contract or the FAR?

You are bound by your individual contract terms, not by the FAR. If your contract references or incorporates sections or clauses of the FAR, then those specific sections or clauses of the FAR may apply to your company. When in doubt, read your contract carefully! If you need help, you can email me at **Christoph@ChristophLLC.com** and complete my online courses at **Courses.ChristophLLC.com**.

INTRODUCTORY CHAPTER 3,
THE CHRISTIAN DOCTRINE AND MISSING GOVERNMENT CONTRACT CLAUSES

What is the Christian doctrine?

First, the Christian doctrine has nothing to do with Christianity or theology. The Christian doctrine is called a doctrine because a judge created it in a court of law. The name "Christian" comes from a famous court case involving a government contractor called G.L. Christian & Associates.

The Christian doctrine is *precedent*, meaning a rule created by a judge that other judges follow in similar cases. This rule says that certain clauses from the Federal Acquisition Regulation (FAR) are so important that the court will pretend as though these clauses are in your government contract, even if the clauses are not actually in the contract you signed. If the Christian doctrine sounds unfair to you, you are paying attention.

When will the Christian doctrine apply?

The official test for the judge to use the Christian doctrine has two parts. The first part asks whether the FAR clause is mandatory. This question asks whether the *prescription clause* instructs the contracting officer to include the clause in the type of contract that your company signed with the government. If the instructions ("prescription") for the clause provide wiggle room or discretion, or if your contract is not appropriate, then the first part of the Christian doctrine fails. If the first or second part of the Christian doctrine fails, the missing clause will not be magically inserted into your government contract.

The second part of the Christian doctrine asks whether the FAR clause expresses a "significant" or "deeply ingrained strand" of government contracting policy. The interpretation of this second part is unpredictable and subjective. The judge gets to decide whether the FAR clause is so important that it cannot be left out of the government contract.

What is the summarized two-part test for applying the Christian doctrine?

In summary, this test for applying the Christian doctrine has two parts. If either part fails, then the judge cannot magically include the missing FAR clause into your government contract.

1. The FAR clause has mandatory instructions to the contracting officer that require its inclusion in the type of government contract you signed.

2. The FAR clause is considered to express a "significant" or "deeply ingrained strand" of government contracting policy. This is extremely subjective.

Does the Christian doctrine apply to subcontracts?

No, the Christian doctrine does not apply to subcontracts or any contracts between two businesses. It applies only to prime contracts of your company with the government.

What if the government contracting officer brings up the Christian doctrine?

Congratulations, your company already wins the argument if the contracting officer starts talking about the Christian doctrine.

Why do you say my company already wins the argument if the contracting officer brings up the Christian doctrine?

The contracting officer forgot to include the FAR clause in your government contract. Months or years later, the contracting officer wants to use this FAR clause against your company, but the FAR clause is not in the contract. Your company points out that this FAR clause is not in the government contract. The contracting officer responds by saying, "Due to the Christian doctrine, this FAR clause is included in the contract by operation of law. You must comply with this FAR clause."

So, the contracting officer thinks you will give up because the gambit of the Christian doctrine sounds legitimate. Do not fall for this bluff! The contracting officer is not a judge.

Who enforces the Christian doctrine?

Remember that the Christian doctrine is created and enforced by judges in courts of law. This means the bluffing contracting officer imagines that two things will happen. First, your company and the government will sue each other and end up in court. Second, the court will apply the Christian doctrine and magically insert the missing FAR clause into your contract. There is a strong chance, however, that one or both things will not happen.

What should I say to the contracting officer during a Christian doctrine situation?

Remind the contracting officer that it will require expensive and time-consuming litigation to get a judge to use the Christian doctrine against your company. The smarter solution is to negotiate in good faith to include the missing clause in your government contract. The government also owes your company extra money to comply with the new FAR clause. Make sure you negotiate a modification that inserts the new FAR clause into the old contract and gives your company more money, if appropriate. For advice with this process, read Part 33, Protests, Disputes, and Appeals.

Is there a list of Christian doctrine clauses?

No, there is no list. There cannot be an exhaustive, official, and complete list because the Christian doctrine is created and enforced by judges in courts of law. Therefore, the list can always expand when the next judge applies the Christian doctrine to a new FAR clause.

However, there are FAR clauses that judges have ruled are covered under the <u>Christian</u> doctrine. These FAR clauses include Disputes, Changes, Termination, and others. Just remember that no list will be complete because a new FAR clause can always enter the mix after a new court case.

INTRODUCTORY CHAPTER 4,
HOW TO RESEARCH FAR CLAUSES

How can I follow changes or updates to the FAR?

All federal regulations, including the FAR, must follow the "public notice and comment" process. This process gives the public advanced, written notice of new and changing regulations and it allows the public to write comments or opinions or objections to send to the regulators.

You can follow changes to federal regulations at the *Federal Register* website. The *Federal Register* posts upcoming proposed and final changes to regulations like the FAR. For most changes to the FAR, you can rely on the secondary reporting and analysis of professionals like Christoph LLC. Email **Christoph@ChristophLLC.com** to sign up for my free, monthly newsletter of important updates in government contracting.

Many law firms and consulting companies publish online articles and updates about major changes to the FAR. You can usually read these for free on the Internet. If you attend government contracting conferences, you can learn the latest and greatest from experts and insiders while you also expand your network of potential teaming partners.

Why does the FAR exist?

Before the FAR, several different sets of government contracting regulations existed. One applied to defense contracts. Another applied to contracts with the National Aeronautics and Space Administration. A third set of regulations applied to contracts with all other federal agencies. This complex arrangement was confusing. In 1984, the FAR was created to create a single set of federal regulations for all government contracts. The FAR replaced the three previous sets of regulations.

What about agency supplements like the DFARS?

Of course, the simplicity of having one set of government contracting regulations did not last. "Nothing gold can stay." Various federal agencies started creating their own, additional, distinct regulations. These regulations supplement (but do not replace) the FAR, so they are called *agency supplements*.

The Department of Defense issues the *Defense FAR Supplement* or *DFARS*. The US Air Force issues the *Air Force FAR Supplement* or *AFFARS*. Scores of other federal agencies issue agency supplements.

Your government contracts may contain clauses from the FAR and also from agency supplements. If you work with defense agencies, you might have to deal with three sets of regulations. For example, a government contract with the Air Force can contain clauses from the FAR, the DFARS, and the AFFARS.

How is the FAR organized?

The FAR is organized into 53 parts. For example, FAR Part 19 covers Small Business Programs. FAR Part 6 covers Competition Requirements. This book is organized into 53 chapters for the 53 parts of the FAR, providing a "highlight reel" of the important issues.

How should I research FAR clauses?

First, make sure you read Part 52 of this book, which explains prescription clauses and the "secret code" of interpreting every single FAR clause. By interpreting the numbers in your FAR clauses, you can tell exactly which part of the FAR explains the policy behind that clause, giving you important context and background. My book is organized according to all 53 parts of the FAR. When you research your FAR clauses, use my book to get the "highlight reel" before you perform an extended analysis of the clause itself and its corresponding FAR part.

If you are not comfortable performing an analysis of *every* FAR clause, term, condition, word, phrase, and requirement in *each* of your government contracts, send me an email at **Christoph@ChristophLLC.com**. I perform such executive summaries for my clients. Maybe I will do it for you! You can also take my online courses about the FAR, available at **Courses.ChristophLLC.com**.

FAR PART 1, FEDERAL ACQUISITION REGULATIONS SYSTEM

FAR Part 1 provides you the basics of how the Federal Acquisition Regulation works, including its purpose, applicability, arrangement, and numbering.

What is the Federal Acquisition Regulation?

The Federal Acquisition Regulation (FAR) is a set of instructions written for federal employees conducting "acquisitions," or buying goods and services. This acquisition process is also called contracting, procurement, purchasing, or "buying stuff."

The FAR explains to the government employees — mostly government contracting officers — what processes to follow when "buying stuff" on behalf of the federal agency. For example, the FAR prescribes which clauses to insert depending on the substance and purpose of a federal contract.

Does the FAR also include the text of the standard clauses the contracting officer is supposed to insert in my government contracts?

Yes, you can find those standard FAR clauses in FAR Part 52, Solicitation Provisions and Contract Clauses.

Is the FAR a set of laws or a set of regulations?

The FAR consists of regulations, which means it is created by federal agencies, as distinguished from laws, which are passed by Congress. However, much of the FAR is based on laws passed by Congress. The FAR "implements" the substance of the law. For example, FAR Part 6, Competition Requirements, implements the substance of a law called the Competition in Contracting Act. FAR Part 19, Small Business Programs, implements the Small Business Act.

What are the guiding principles of the FAR?

The guiding principles of the FAR are as follows:

Satisfy the federal client in terms of cost, quality, and delivery.
Maximize the use of commercial products and commercial services.
Select contractors with good past performance or the ability to perform.
Promote competition among contractors.
Conduct business with integrity, fairness, and transparency.
Fulfill government policy objectives.

What is the most interesting section in the FAR?

The most interesting section is FAR 1.102(d), which states the following:

> "In exercising initiative, government members of the acquisition team may assume if a specific strategy, practice, policy, or procedure is in the best interests of the government and is not addressed in the FAR, nor prohibited by law (statute or case law), executive order, or other regulation, that the strategy, practice, policy, or procedure is a permissible exercise of authority."

What does FAR 1.102(d) mean in plain English?

In plain English, FAR 1.102(d) means the government can do things differently and innovate if nothing prohibits the new way of doing business. Unless you find something that says you cannot do so, go ahead and try out new ideas that benefit the government. This section encourages positive changes to government contracting.

This process sounds quite different from the rigid, over-regulated, complicated mess that is the usual government contracting. Many contracting officers do not know about this section of the FAR. Many fear using this authority because it requires initiative and risk taking. If you have great ideas for improving the process or doing things in a completely new and different way, send your ideas to the government along with the text of FAR 1.102(d).

To whom does the FAR apply?

The FAR applies to federal employees conducting acquisitions, a function otherwise known as contracting, procurement, purchasing, or "buying stuff." The FAR is written primarily for contracting officers, who have the authority to sign, modify, administer, and terminate contracts on behalf of the federal government.

Does the FAR apply to government contractors?

No, but that does not mean that the FAR is not *relevant* to government contractors! For a full explanation, read Introductory Chapter 2, "No, the FAR Does Not Apply to Government Contractors."

Where can I find the official text of the FAR?

The official, online source of the FAR is **www.acquisition.gov**, which is maintained by the General Services Administration. However, I must warn you: I have found several errors over the years in this "official" source. For that reason, although **www.acquisition.gov** is convenient and easy to use, I do not trust it fully.

Another official source for any regulation, including the FAR, is the electronic *Code of Federal Regulations,* available online at **www.ecfr.gov**. Many other websites reproduce the FAR or discuss the FAR. Just remember that the official website for the FAR is **www.acquisition.gov** and the official website for all regulations, including the FAR, is **www.ecfr.gov**.

What is the Code of Federal Regulations?

The *Code of Federal Regulations (CFR)* is the organized set of all federal regulations, including the FAR. The CFR is organized by titles and chapter. The FAR is Chapter 1 of Title 48 of the CFR.

Should I read the FAR in a printed, hardcopy book?

No, printed books that reproduce the text of the FAR are a waste of trees. Do not rely on books or hard copies of the full text of the FAR. Printed versions of the FAR quickly become outdated because the FAR constantly changes. If you buy a book that reprints the text of the FAR, that book is likely obsolete and inaccurate soon after the ink dries. Do not buy such books. Instead, send an extra copy of this book to someone who needs it.

How is the FAR organized?

The FAR is organized into 53 parts. Each part is further divided into subparts, sections, and subsections. You only need to understand the level of detail for parts of the FAR. For example, FAR Part 19 covers Small Business Programs. FAR Part 6 covers Competition Requirements. This book gives you a plain-English summary of all 53 FAR parts.

What part of the FAR matters most to my government contracting company?

The most important part is FAR Part 52, which contains the standard contract clauses.

Is there a pattern I can recognize in every single FAR clause in my government contract?

A simple pattern applies to all FAR clauses, telling you the origin and purpose of each FAR clause. Every FAR clause starts with 52 because all FAR clauses are found in FAR Part 52. After the number 52, every FAR clause has a period or dot, then three numbers, then a dash, then more numbers. Pay attention to the first three numbers after the period.

Why should I pay attention to the first three numbers after the period in the FAR clause?

Of those three numbers, the first will be the number two. That detail is not important. But the second and third numbers tell you something very important about the FAR clause.

What do the second and third numbers indicate?

If the FAR clause starts with 52.219, that clause derives from FAR Part 19, Small Business Programs. Ignore the 52 and ignore the number two after the period. You are left with 19, which tells you that FAR clause comes from FAR Part 19, Small Business Programs. Another example is a FAR clause that starts with 52.249. Any FAR clause that starts with 52.249 derives from FAR Part 49, Termination of Contracts.

Why should I care about the FAR Part that corresponds to the FAR clause?

Each FAR clause has specific directions to the contracting officer about when to insert the clause. This detail helps you understand the purpose of the FAR clause and gives you negotiating leverage if you want to remove it before signing the contract. You can look up these directions and debate whether the clause belongs in your contract. Read more in Part 52, Solicitation Provisions and Contract Clauses.

What is an imperative sentence?

Imperative sentences issue commands or instructions. In plain English, imperative sentences tell you what to do!

What are some examples of imperative sentences?

"Do this!" "Don't do that!" "The contracting officer shall document the file." "The contractor shall notify the contracting officer."

How should you interpret imperative sentences within the FAR?

If you read an "imperative sentence" in the FAR, or a sentence that requires action, the general rule is that the contracting officer is responsible for this action. Unless another person or party is expressly listed as responsible, the contracting officer is responsible by default.

What is a delegation?

If a higher level official delegates a duty, responsibility, or power to a subordinate official, we call that a *delegation*. For example, the contracting officer delegates some contract administration powers to the contracting officer's representative (COR).

Can the duties, responsibilities, or powers listed within the FAR be delegated?

The general rule of the FAR is that any authority is delegable unless specifically stated otherwise. Powers, responsibilities, and duties can be delegated, or passed down to a subordinate official, unless the FAR explicitly forbids it.

With so many different definitions in the FAR, how can I know which definition applies?

FAR Part 2, Definitions of Words and Terms contains a set of definitions that apply to the entire FAR. You can use these definitions in any other section or part of the FAR, unless you find a more specific definition of the same word in another section or part of the FAR.

For example, the FAR Part 2 definition of "day" applies, generally, throughout the entire FAR. However, FAR Part 33, Protests, Disputes, and Appeals has a more specific definition for "day." By following this convention, we know that when we read within that section of FAR Part 33, we must follow the definition of "day" as found in FAR Part 33, not the definition of "day" found in FAR Part 2. For more information, read Part 2, Definitions of Words and Terms.

How should I calculate dollar thresholds listed in the FAR?

Understanding the convention for dollar thresholds is important. As a contracting professional, you will need to track and follow many different dollar thresholds. Unless otherwise stated, all dollar thresholds apply to the entire transaction, including all options. Let's look at an example.

Let's agree that the FAR dollar threshold for requiring contractors to show notarized proof is "any contract greater than or equal to $5 million." Your company just signed a contract with the Department of Defense. The contract is for five years, for $1 million per year. When you sign the contract, only the first year is obligated and funded for $1 million. The later four years are optional because the government has the option to exercise those periods of performance. If the government exercises every single option, the entire contract will total $5 million. But at the onset, you can expect only $1 million of payment.

Even though you signed a contract for the first year for only $1 million, because of the remaining option periods, the dollar threshold for this transaction is $5 million, not $1 million. You need to count all possible options when calculating the dollar threshold. Therefore, in this example, your company is required to provide notarized proof.

Does the FAR reference other regulations, or other laws, or other policies?

Yes, sometimes the FAR references other forms of government contracting regulations, laws passed by Congress, or policies issued by executive agencies.

What if the law referenced in the FAR has been amended or changed over time?

When the FAR cites other laws, regulations, or policies, the citation includes any amendments, unless otherwise stated. This convention saves time by avoiding FAR revisions every time the law changes.

What is a deviation?

A *deviation* occurs when the government breaks the rules of the FAR in any one of several specific ways, such as the following:

Including a contract clause that is inconsistent with the FAR
Including a solicitation provision that is inconsistent with the FAR
Failing to include a clause or provision when the FAR requires it
Using unauthorized, "modified" versions of clauses or provisions

Think of a deviation as a limitation of the power of federal agencies, which are supposed to follow the FAR. If the agency starts "homebrewing" its own FAR clauses, this practice diminishes the authority of the FAR system and creates confusion in the government contracting industry.

Are deviations ever allowable?

Yes, agencies can deviate from the FAR, but only when the head of the agency authorizes the deviation in writing. So, deviations should be purposeful, not accidental.

What is the difference between individual deviations and class deviations?

Individual deviations affect only one contract. Class deviations affect more than one contract, possibly even an entire group or category of contracts. For example, an agency might use a class deviation from the FAR for all contracts for services greater than $100 million. If the agency expects to use the class deviation on a permanent basis, rather than as a temporary fix, the agency should propose a formal, permanent revision to the FAR, rather than using a class deviation.

Can deviations quickly implement changes in laws created by Congress?

Yes, deviations help agencies to react quickly to legislative changes. Although agencies need months or years to change the FAR formally, an agency can issue deviations in just a few days.

When Congress passes a government contracting law that is too important to wait months or years to implement in the FAR, agencies can quickly issue a deviation while they wait for the formal revision to the FAR. Once the FAR is formally revised, the deviation is no longer valid or necessary. In this way, agencies can quickly implement legislative changes, like the annual law called the *National Defense Authorization Act* or *NDAA*.

What is an unauthorized commitment?

Only contracting officers have the authority to sign contracts on behalf of the federal government. Contracting officer authority flows from a written warrant, which specifies any dollar limitation. For example, one contracting officer may hold a warrant to sign any contract that is $50 million or less.

An *unauthorized commitment* means an agreement that is *not binding* because the government representative who made it lacks the authority to enter into that agreement. Therefore, the agreement is not valid and is not an enforceable contract. For example, the agency program manager may have cut a deal with a contractor, but the program manager is not a contracting officer and holds no warrant. Therefore, whatever agreement the program manager created, negotiated, or signed is invalid, and is not an enforceable contract. Rather, the agreement is called an *unauthorized commitment*.

Can a contracting officer create an unauthorized commitment?

Yes, even a warranted contracting officer can create an unauthorized commitment. Contracting officers must be careful to sign contracts only within the scope of their limited warrant. For example, a contracting officer with a warrant to sign any contract that is $50 million or less cannot sign a contract for $200 million. If that contracting officer signs a $200 million contract, that agreement is an *unauthorized commitment*.

How can agencies "fix" problems created by an unauthorized commitment?

If the agency wants to honor and validate the unauthorized commitment, the agency can execute a *ratification*.

What is a ratification?

A *ratification* is the formal process whereby an agency "fixes" an unauthorized commitment using the approval of a federal employee who has the authority to sign the original contract.

Are ratifications rare, or are ratifications common?

Ratifications are rare because they are embarrassing to the federal agency. Processing a ratification draws attention to a serious mistake by the agency. Sometimes federal employees are punished for unauthorized commitments.

What is a determination and findings (D&F)?

A *determination and findings* (D&F) is a formal memo in a special format, signed by the appropriate federal employee, who is often the contracting officer. Some actions or decisions require a D&F to document that the contracting officer thoroughly examined and considered the action or decision. In the D&F, the "determination" (conclusion, decision to act) is supported by the "findings" (facts, data, or evidence).

How can I learn more practical, real-world advice about the FAR?

Complete my online courses available at **Courses.ChristophLLC.com.**

FAR Part 2, Definitions of Words and Terms

FAR Part 2 provides a set of definitions that apply throughout the FAR unless another section uses a more specific definition for that same word.

Is it possible for the same word to have different definitions within the FAR?

Yes! You must understand that in many cases, the FAR can have many different definitions *for the very same word*. Depending on how you use that word, or what section of the FAR applies, the definition changes. For example, there are more than 20 different definitions for "subcontract" throughout the FAR.

If I find a word defined in FAR Part 2, but that word is also defined differently in another section of the FAR, how do I proceed?

If you find a conflict between the *general* definition in FAR Part 2 and a different definition in another section or part of the FAR, use that definition found within that other section or part. Defer to the different definition in any section or part other than FAR Part 2, when you are interpreting within that other section or part. If the section or part has no definition of the word, you can use the general definition in FAR Part 2.

What process should I follow to make sure I always use the correct definition within the FAR?

Step 1: Determine what section or part of the FAR you are interpreting.

Step 2: Determine what word you need defined.

Step 3: Search for a definition of that word (from Step 2) in the section or part of the FAR (from Step 1). If you find a definition, stop right there! Use that definition.

Step 4: If you find no definition during Step 3, search for a definition of that word in FAR Part 2, Definitions of Words and Terms. If you find a definition only in FAR Part 2—and no definition exists in the section or part of the FAR you are interpreting—you can use the *general* definition found in FAR Part 2.

Example:

Step 1: We will interpret within FAR 33.1, Protests.

Step 2: We will define the word "day."

Step 3: We find a definition of the word "day" within FAR 33.1. Great! We will use the definition of "day" found in FAR 33.1, even though there is a different definition of "day" found in FAR Part 2, Definitions of Words and Terms. The definition of "day" in FAR 33.1 trumps the *general* definition of "day" found in FAR Part 2.

Should I define terms in my prime contract or subcontract?

Yes, you should define as many relevant terms as possible. Create a "definitions" section. Defining your terms will avoid future disagreements.

What type of disagreements can my company avoid by defining terms in contracts?

An *ambiguity* is when two or more reasonable interpretations for the same word, phrase, or concept exists. Since one goal of signing a contract is to arrive at a "meeting of the minds" and a mutual agreement, ambiguities in a contract represent a failure to achieve this goal. Eliminate possible ambiguities by defining the terms in the contract (or subcontract).

FAR Part 3, Improper Business Practices and Personal Conflicts of Interest

FAR Part 3 covers the ethical rules of government contracting, including conflicts of interest.

I have a question concerning ethics, conflicts of interest, improper business practices, and other such topics. What should I do?

You need to get a legal opinion from your company's attorney, or you need to ask for a legal opinion from the agency's attorney or ethics official. Remember, my book is not legal advice. Hire an attorney for legal advice.

What is a conflict of interest?

The classic case of a conflict of interest is when you serve two masters. Your loyalty to one master conflicts with your loyalty to the other master. For example, you're suing another company over a government contracting dispute. Would you want to have the same attorney as the other company? In another example, let's say you're buying a house. Would you want your buyer's agent to be the same person as the agent representing the seller? In both cases, the attorney or real estate agent has a classic conflict of interest.

Can you provide a classic example of a conflict of interest in government contracting?

Sure, let's say your company provides onsite support services for a federal agency. Your employees assist the government contracting officer in designing the statement of work and crafting the request for proposals for a multi-million-dollar contract for project XYZ. Your company has a classic conflict of interest if it wants to submit a proposal for project XYZ.

Since your employees helped to write the statement of work and request for proposals, they have insider information about project XYZ that your competitors do not have. Since your employees' government contract requires them to support the federal client, their dual loyalty to your company creates a conflict of interest between the federal client and their employer (your company). Your employees may write the statement of work or request for proposals in a way that favors your company. Your employees may "leak" — purposefully or accidentally — insider information that will give your company an unfair advantage in the competition. In this situation, your company has a classic "organizational conflict of interest" in competing for project XYZ.

Why do conflicts of interest matter in government contracting?

Federal agencies spend taxpayer money on federal contracts, meaning agencies have a special duty to protect the interest of taxpayers. For this reason, the ethics rules for government contracting are stricter than for private-sector business deals. Government business must be conducted in a manner "above reproach," with "complete impartiality," and with "preferential treatment for none." The government's policy is to avoid any conflicts of interest *or even the appearance* of a conflict of interest in government-contractor relationships.

What can my company do to avoid or mitigate conflicts of interest?

Create a written *Code of Business Ethics and Conduct* and tailor your documents to comply with government contracting policy. Designate an "ethics official" for your company, who is responsible for all such issues, including fielding questions from your employees.

Provide your employees thorough and regular training about ethics. Train your employees to recognize when the work they perform may "conflict out" your company (may prevent your company from proposing to win an upcoming government contract because of a conflict of interest). If necessary, set up "firewalls" (physical or abstract separations or preventative measures) between your employees who perform onsite support services versus employees who write proposals and develop new business (win contracts). If you do not have a qualified expert on staff, hire an outside consultant to help you with these processes. You can email me at **Christoph@ChristophLLC.com**.

Are there any types of government contracting work that require additional training or scrutiny?

If you have employees who perform services onsite or in support of the government, especially related to contracting or acquisitions functions, these employees may require further training and scrutiny. Also beware any employees who support government clients performing inherently governmental functions (read more about this topic in Part 7, Acquisition Planning).

What are some examples of employees who require additional training or scrutiny?

Keep an eye on employees who perform support services — for the government client — related to any acquisition or contracting functions, such as:

Acquisition planning
Developing statements of work
Determining what the government should buy
Developing any contracting documentation
Evaluating proposals
Awarding, administering, modifying, and terminating contracts
Determining whether contract costs are reasonable, allowable, and allocable

If you have employees supporting the contracting, finance, legal, engineering, or program office — or any function related to acquisition or contracting — you must be extra cautious. These types of onsite support services often generate conflicts of interest and create access to insider information.

Are bribes, gifts, or gratuities appropriate in government contracting?

No, absolutely not! Never provide any bribes, gifts, or gratuities to any government employee. Do not even think about it!

But we always send gifts to our clients. Every year, we send a fruit basket to each supplier. Any account over $1 million gets tickets for the regional sports team's executive suite. What is the problem?

No, no, no! Although giving gifts to clients is normal in the private sector, this practice is forbidden in government contracting. Do not give gifts of any type to your government clients.

Are federal employees subject to any financial scrutiny?

Yes, federal employees involved in government contracting must disclose (report) their financial and investment information every year.

Are contractors protected by any of these ethical rules for government contracting?

Yes, *contractor bid or proposal information* and proprietary information is protected by several laws and regulations, including the *Procurement Integrity Act*. When your company provides its proprietary pricing information to the government, perhaps as part of a proposal, the government is required to safeguard it.

What is contractor bid or proposal information?

Contractor bid or proposal information includes cost or pricing data, direct labor rates, indirect labor rates, and proprietary information about your business processes, operations, or techniques. Protect your financial and pricing information!

How can I increase the chances that my proprietary information will be protected?

Always mark your proprietary information. Your company must have standard operating procedures for marking proprietary information. Your employees must be trained to mark the information appropriately.

What if I think my competitor is violating these ethical rules — can I report the violation?

Yes, you can report suspected violations of any of the ethical rules to the contracting officer or the *agency ethics official* (usually an attorney for the agency that specializes in contracting ethics). Both the contracting officer and agency ethics official have a duty to investigate the matter and take appropriate action.

Are there prohibitions against government contractors colluding on price?

Yes, colluding with your competitors is a serious, possibly criminal violation. Almost every government contracting competition requires your company to certify that it arrived at its price independently (without colluding with any other companies).

Where in the contract did my company certify about independent pricing?

Search for "Certificate of Independent Price Determination."

Why is the Procurement Integrity Act important for government contractors?

If your pricing, financial, or other proprietary information were released to your competitors, your company would encounter substantial problems. Your competitors could undercut your pricing or steal your "secret sauce." For these reasons, the *Procurement Integrity Act* restricts the government from releasing your proprietary information. In addition to protecting your proprietary information, the Procurement Integrity Act also protects government source selection sensitive information.

What is the difference between proprietary information versus source selection sensitive information?

Ask yourself who cares more about protecting the information. You can easily distinguish between proprietary information versus source selection sensitive information. Both are protected from improper disclosure by the Procurement Integrity Act. However, controlling proprietary information protects your company. Controlling source selection sensitive information protects the government's selection process.

For example, the names of government source selection decisionmakers and the draft version of a proposal evaluation are both source selection sensitive. The names and draft provide intimate details about the government's selection process. In contrast, your company's pricing and financial details are proprietary information. Spreading this information will hurt your company.

In government contracting, does my company have a duty to protect proprietary information of my competitors?

Yes, according to the Procurement Integrity Act. The government must protect your proprietary information. In turn, you must protect proprietary or sensitive information, even if you receive it only by mistake.

What should I do if I receive my competitor's proprietary information by mistake?

Do not seek an advantage if you receive your competitor's proprietary information by mistake. That decision would be unethical and possibly violate the Procurement Integrity Act. It is not worth the risk. Instead, you must acknowledge the mistake, inform everyone, and try to fix the situation.

Remember that the rules of government contracting differ from the rules of business for other industries. Other industries may allow you to use information that accidentally "falls into your lap." This is not the case in government contracting. The Procurement Integrity Act forbids your company from taking advantage of proprietary information from your competitor.

Should I delete the email, or should I acknowledge the mistake?

You should acknowledge the mistake and inform the government, immediately.

Let's say the government accidentally emails you the proposal of your competitor. Your competitor's proposal contains proprietary information, such as individual labor rates, indirect rates, and the total price of your competitor's offer. This information is extremely valuable for you, but you must resist the temptation to take advantage. The Procurement Integrity Act sets up a strict protocol for your company to follow.

First step: Acknowledge the mistake. Notify both the government contracting officer and your competitor (whose information you mistakenly received). Notify both parties in writing.

Why is it important to act quickly after my company accidentally receives proprietary information?

The reason you should act quickly is that the longer you wait, the more it seems like your company was trying to take advantage of this mistake. What if the government investigates months later? Any gap between when you received the information and when you acknowledged the mistake seems like evidence that your company did something wrong. Move quickly.

How should my company document the mistake and steps to correct it?

Second step: Write and sign a memorandum for record that explains how your company corrected the error. Be transparent. Name those people who have seen the documents. Explain how your company deleted or shredded all copies of the document. Include your information technology specialist to describe how the documents were deleted altogether from your network or server. Your company's leadership should sign this memo and provide a copy to the government.

What two government officials should my company notify?

Coordinate and cooperate completely with both the contracting officer and the agency ethics official, who is likely to be an attorney in the legal office. Request in writing to be connected to the agency ethics official so you can make sure that you follow all required procedures.

FAR Part 4, Administrative and Information Matters

FAR Part 4 describes the administrative aspects of contract execution, including distribution, signatures, numbering, reporting, file retention, and the Federal Procurement Data System.

What is a Procurement Instrument Identifier (PIID)?

Procurement Instrument Identifier or *PIID* is a fancy name for the contract number. Most federal government contract numbers look like this:

AA1234-20-A-0005

Six characters, a dash, two numbers, a dash, one letter, a dash, followed by four numbers. You may find the entire contract number written with no dashes.

The first six characters (in my example, "AA1234") identifies the contract office. Each contract office has its own set of six characters, often consisting of two letters and four numbers.

The second set of two numbers (in my example, "20") refers to the fiscal year during which the contract was signed. If you see "20," that contract was signed in fiscal year 2020. If you see "15," that contract was signed in fiscal year 2015. Remember, the government's fiscal year starts October 1 and ends September 30.

The single letter (in my example, "A") gives you a clue about the contract type.

Finally, the last set of four numbers (in my example, "0005") is a numerical counter for agency convenience. The first contract of that fiscal year will end with "0001." The second contract will end with "0002," and so on.

Who has the authority to sign contracts on behalf of the federal government?

Contracting officers! Also, the head of a federal agency has inherent power to sign contracts on behalf of the agency, but agency heads usually delegate this power to the contracting officers.

Most contracts require two signatures: one by the contracting officer, one on behalf of the contractor. Who signs first?

The contracting officer normally signs the contract after it has been signed by the contractor. So, typically, the contractor signs first.

Who should sign contracts on behalf of my company?

Anyone with the authority to bind your company contractually can sign the government contract. My recommendation is that your company create a policy that one specific person be solely responsible for signing all government contracts.

Should I sign my legal name, or the company's legal name?

Remember that your contract with the government is with your company, not with you personally. For that reason, you should type the name of your company (because you are signing on behalf of the company). Then you should type your name and your job title as it relates to the company. For example, you could sign your name above this text:

> Acme Manufacturing North America, LLC
> Cornelius Stark, Managing Member

If you run a sole proprietorship or if you will sign the contract as an individual, then maybe you sign and type only your name. However, be careful. Consider forming a company (corporation, limited liability company, etc.) rather than operating as an individual or sole proprietorship. Of course, you should consult a business attorney and tax professional when making these decisions.

Does the contracting officer have a duty to distribute copies of the signed contract or modification?

Yes. Within 10 working days after everyone signs, the contracting officer is supposed to send your company a copy of the executed contract or modification. Expect your copy to be sent by email.

Why should I expect the copy of my signed contract or modification to be sent via email?

The federal government's policy is to use electronic commerce (which includes email) whenever practicable or cost-effective. In fact, when you read the FAR, you may find terms like "copy," "document," "page," etc., but you should not interpret that to mean you will receive or work with printed paper copies.

What is the Federal Procurement Data System (FPDS)?

The *Federal Procurement Data System (FPDS)* is a public database of government contract actions. Various data elements about *contract actions* are available on the FPDS website, which is **www.fpds.gov**.

Who uses the data in FPDS?

Congress, the Government Accountability Office, the President of the United States, and other federal agencies monitor and analyze the data in FPDS to track various policy goals. For example, the Small Business Administration can generate reports on the percentage of government contracts awarded to small businesses, women-owned small businesses (WOSB), or other categories. Congress can analyze FPDS reports to determine how many contracts are awarded with or without competition.

Can or should I look at the data in FPDS?

Yes, you can and should use FPDS, which is a free resource, available to anyone with an Internet connection. You can search FPDS to see what types of contracts your competitors hold, what your potential federal clients are buying, and how much money is spent on the goods or services in your target market. FPDS is a powerful resource for open-source intelligence, market research, and competitive analysis.

Who reports data to FPDS?

Contracting officers are required to report certain data elements for every *contract action*. The contracting officers certify a *contract action report* or *CAR*.

What qualifies as a "contract action" that is reportable in FPDS?

A *contract action* is any oral or written action that results in the government spending appropriated money in an amount greater than the micro-purchase threshold, and also modifications thereof. *Appropriated money* means money that Congress authorized and appropriated the agency to spend. The *micro-purchase threshold* is a dollar figure that changes periodically. You can find the definition (current dollar value) of the micro-purchase threshold in FAR Part 2, Definitions of Words and Terms.

Do modifications count as contract actions?

Yes, modifications to contracts count as contract actions that must be reported to FPDS.

What about different types of government agreements that are not traditional, FAR-based contracts? Do those other types of agreements count as contract actions?

No, grants, cooperative agreements, "Other Transactions" (for research or prototypes), real property leases, requisitions from federal stock, and training authorizations do not count as contract actions. Therefore, according to FAR Part 4, they are not reportable to FPDS. You should know that some agencies, like the Department of Defense, report some Other Transactions in FPDS, but this practice is not mandated by the FAR.

How long should a contractor keep records of government contracts?

If you wish, you can carefully read through FAR Part 4 to find out the various retention periods (how long you must keep your files available for inspection). You will find that some documents must be retained for 3 years, or 6 years, or some other length of time. My recommendation is to keep all your government contracting files for at least 6 years after you think the contract is completed, paid, and "closed out."

Why should I keep my files for 6 years? Why should I keep any files longer than the minimum length of time?

The reason I recommend you retain your files for a minimum of 6 years is because any formal claim under the Contract Disputes Act must be filed within 6 years of when you knew or should have known about the basis of the claim. So, my advice is practical. Keep your government contract files for at least 6 years.

At least 6 years from when? From when the contract is signed, or from when the contract is completed?

Six years from when the contract is completed, paid, and you reasonably believe there are no outstanding issues, such as cost reconciliations, audits, or outstanding claims. Remember, many government contracts have a potential period of performance of 5 years. If you start the clock at contract signature, you will retain your documents for just 1 year after the end of the last period of performance. Five years later, you arrived at the end of the period of performance, and you retained your files for an additional year. Potentially, this practice is a big mistake!

You have 6 years from the time you knew or should have known about the basis of the claim to file a formal claim under the Contract Disputes Act. If the basis of the claim started during the last year of the 5-year contract, you want to have all those files on hand if you discover or decide you have a claim a few years later.

Should I store my government contracting files electronically or in paper copies?

If your company uses paper files instead of digital storage, I wish you "Good luck." You will need it. Digital storage is cheaper, faster, and easier. I prefer digital storage. I have worked in federal agencies that use paper contracts, and I have worked in federal agencies that use digital contracts. I am certain that digital storage is superior.

FAR Part 5, Publicizing Contract Actions

FAR Part 5 prescribes policy for publicizing contract actions to increase competition.

What counts as a "contract action" in FAR Part 5?

Within FAR Part 5, a *contract action* is an action resulting in a *new* federal contract. In this context, modifications to an existing federal contract do not count as a contract action.

But wait! In FAR Part 4, Administrative and Information Matters, the definition of "contract action" includes modifications. Why is the definition different in FAR Part 5?

As a reminder, many words have different definitions within different sections of the FAR. You must carefully consider the application of any definition you discover. Go back and re-read Part 2, Definitions of Words and Terms.

What is the government's policy for publicizing contract actions (new contracts) and contract opportunities?

Contracting officers must publicize new contracts to increase competition, encourage wider participation in the federal contracting industry, and help small businesses (and the other subsets of small businesses, like women-owned small businesses) win contracts and subcontracts.

Therefore, the government wants you to know about new contracts, or the solicitations for new contracts, so you can submit a proposal. Also, the government publicizes contracts so you can team up with the prime contractor by working as a subcontractor. Increased competition (more proposals) means the government gets superior results at favorable prices.

FAR Part 5 mentions the "governmentwide point of entry" — what is that?

When you read *governmentwide point of entry* or *GPE*, that phrase refers to the government's official website for publicizing contracts and solicitations. The official website is *System for Award Management (SAM)*. The website address is **www.sam.gov**. The previous website was called Federal Business Opportunities (FBO). When the government transitioned from FBO to SAM, the interim website called "Beta.SAM" was located at **www.beta.sam.gov**.

Why should you care about SAM and the so-called governmentwide point of entry?

The official website is your official source for finding new contract opportunities. Although you can subscribe to paid services that filter, organize, or highlight data about new contract opportunities, the originating source for these services is SAM.

You can pay for services that make searching for contracts easier, or you can perform this research on your own, for free, using the official government website. You can easily create a free account.

Much like the Federal Procurement Data System or FPDS (described in FAR Part 4, Administrative and Information Matters), the System for Award Management is a powerful resource for free market research, competitive analysis, and open-source intelligence. Bookmark these websites and practice navigating them. You can search for government contracts by location, federal agency, type of work, and many other search terms.

Can contractors submit contract opportunities to SAM?

Yes, prime contractors can submit notices of subcontracting opportunities to attract potential subcontractors. Even subcontractors can submit notices for further (lower-tier) subcontracting opportunities. These notices of subcontracting opportunities should include a description of the business opportunity, any prequalification requirements, and a contact or resource for learning more about the technical requirements.

Why would a contractor let its competitors know about a contract opportunity?

Great question! In government contracting, your competitors are also potential teaming partners, and your teaming partners are also potential competitors. When your company cannot perform as the prime contractor, you need to team up with another company by performing as its subcontractor. When your company cannot perform *all* the work as the prime contractor, you need to find another company to perform as your subcontractor.

Broaden your horizons. Expand your network to increase your potential pool of teaming partners, including prime contractors and subcontractors.

FAR Part 6, Competition Requirements

FAR Part 6 explains the different levels of competition and provides instructions for limiting competition by issuing a Justification and Approval (J&A).

What is full and open competition?

Full and open competition refers to the government's default standard for allowing all responsible, registered companies or individuals to submit proposals for contracts. Basically, if your company is in good standing and registered in the System for Award Management, you are eligible to win government contracts solicited under full and open competition.

What is the most common procedure for a full and open competition?

Full and open competition usually follows the familiar process of issuing a solicitation, usually in the form of a *Request for Proposals (RFP)*. Your company submits a proposal, which will be evaluated against a set of factors like price, past performance, or technical approach.

Can my company protest a decision made under full and open competition?

Yes. In fact, your company has the most "rights" or protections under full and open competition. Since this is the highest level of competition required of the government, it has the highest number of rules that cannot be broken. If these rules are broken, however, your company may be able to protest the contract award formally at the agency, Government Accountability Office, or Court of Federal Claims.

What is full and open competition after exclusion of sources?

Full and open competition allows (basically) any company to compete. In contrast, *full and open competition after exclusion of sources* allows any company *within certain categories* to compete.

Is a small business set-aside an example of full and open competition after exclusion of sources?

Yes, the most common example of using full and open competition after exclusion of sources is when the government solicits a contract as a *small business set-aside*. When only small businesses are eligible to compete for the contract, we have full and open competition *but only among small businesses*. The "exclusion of sources" refers to all the large businesses that are ineligible to compete.

Another example is when the government solicits a contract as a *women-owned small business (WOSB) set-aside*. In this example, the excluded sources include all large businesses and also small businesses that do not qualify as WOSB.

Yet another example is when the government restricts award to local companies after a major disaster or emergency. By excluding any companies not in the disaster area, the government helps the local economy recover by stimulating local businesses.

Apart from set-asides or preference for local companies, the government has one more reason to exclude certain sources. Sometimes the government wants to create or maintain alternative sources, so the government decides to "spread the wealth." By excluding certain sources, the government "spreads the wealth" to alternative sources.

For example, company XYZ wins 90 percent of the contracts for medical devices. By excluding company XYZ, the government diversifies its supplier base for medical devices. The other companies receive more contracts, increase their revenue, and expand their market share to become an alternative source for the government.

How can this process be full and open competition if entire categories of companies can be excluded — as in a small business set-aside?

So many names and concepts in the FAR are confusing or misleading, which is one reason why I wrote this book. Just remember that full and open competition after exclusion of sources is a method of solicitation that allows competition *only among a certain class of companies,* for example, small businesses, women-owned small businesses, or local firms in a disaster area.

What types of contracting procedures qualify as full and open competition?

FAR Part 6 lists the following as methods of contract competition that satisfy the requirements of full and open competition: sealed bidding, competitive proposals, combinations of competitive procedures (such as two-step sealed bidding), and *other competitive procedures.*

Other competitive procedures (that also satisfy full and open competition) include the following: selection of sources under architect-engineer contracts using the procedures of the Brooks Act, orders from General Services Administration (GSA) Schedule contracts, and Broad Agency Announcements (BAA) for research that use peer or scientific review for selection decisions.

What is other than full and open competition? Is other than full and open competition different from full and open competition after exclusion of sources?

Yes, you must understand that "full and open competition" and "full and open competition after exclusion of sources" can be grouped together as two forms of competitive procedures. Now we can discuss the third category, which is *noncompetitive.* This third category is called *other than full and open competition.*

Is other than full and open competition related to sole-source contracts?

Yes, a *sole-source contract* is one example of using *other than full and open competition*. Congress provided specific exceptions where federal agencies do not have to follow competitive procedures. To make sure agencies do not abuse this special authority, Congress requires agencies to state the reason specifically for their using other than full and open competition.

How must federal agencies specifically state the reason for using other than full and open competition?

You may hear the term *J&A* or *justification and approval*. This justification document outlines why the government will not or cannot satisfy the standard of full and open competition. Another name for the J&A is *justification for other than full and open competition*. What a mouthful!

The J&A will specifically reference the reason the government is not using full and open competition. There are only seven categories—seven acceptable reasons—for issuing a J&A and using other than full and open competition.

What are the seven acceptable reasons for the government to issue a J&A for other than full and open competition?

This mnemonic device will help you to remember the seven reasons for a J&A or justification and approval for other than full and open competition: IOUSNIP. Each of the letters stands for a possible reason for issuing the J&A. The most common reason is "sole source," which is "only one source" in the mnemonic device, IOUSNIP. Here's the complete list:

International agreement
Only one source
Urgency
Statute (a specific law)
National security

Industrial mobilization
Public interest

International agreement means a treaty with a foreign country requires a particular vendor to win the government contract. The term *only one source* is self-explanatory. Only one source can perform the service or deliver the product. *Urgency* means an unusual and compelling urgency threatens serious injury to the government. Lack of planning does not count!

Statute means that a law passed by Congress requires a particular vendor to win the government contract. *National security* is a vague reason that can mean almost anything, depending on your opinion.

Industrial mobilization means the government needs to bolster specific industries or certain technological capabilities. Therefore, the government will award contracts to certain companies to keep this industry strong or influence it toward new priorities. Finally, *public interest* is a vague excuse that can be abused easily. What is the public interest? You tell me! Let's argue for a few hours. To protect against overuse of the public interest exception, federal agencies must notify Congress if they intend to use public interest to avoid full and open competition.

Can you challenge the J&A?

If your company gets a government contract due to a J&A, consider yourself lucky. If your company cannot compete for a government contract because of a J&A, you can challenge the validity of the J&A. The J&A will be posted to the Internet, so you can examine it.

Although you can try to challenge the J&A to force the government to compete the contract, you are likely to fail. Successful challenges to a J&A are rare. A better strategy is to communicate with the government before it issues the J&A. Convince the government that your company can also deliver the services or product. Your intervention may persuade the government to open the contract to full and open competition.

What are some unacceptable reasons for using other than full and open competition (noncompetitive contracts)?

The FAR specifically forbids agencies from using these two excuses:

Unacceptable excuse number one: "My agency ran out of time, so we issued a noncompetitive contract using other than full and open competition." Lack of advance planning is never a valid excuse for using noncompetitive procedures.

Unacceptable excuse number two: "My agency funding is expiring soon, and my agency does not want to wait for next year's money to arrive to award this contract, so I don't have time for competitive procedures." This poor excuse is based on the time-limited nature of agency funding. Again, lack of planning is never a valid excuse for using noncompetitive procedures.

FAR Part 7, Acquisition Planning

FAR Part 7 explains how the government makes acquisition decisions and what qualifies as inherently governmental functions.

What is acquisition planning?

Acquisition planning is the government process of thinking carefully about the best way to purchase and maintain whatever the government buys, including the full life-cycle cost.

What does life-cycle cost mean?

Life-cycle cost means the *total cost* for the government of acquiring, operating, supporting, maintaining, and eventually disposing of whatever the government buys. The important concept is that the government's total cost does not stop after the contract is signed, or even after the contract period of performance is completed.

For complex purchases, such as multi-million-dollar programs, the life-cycle costs can span decades. The cost of supporting or maintaining major weapons systems can be several multiples of the upfront purchase price. You can compare this process to the life-cycle cost of your car. In addition to the purchase price of the car, you must pay for parking, maintenance, repairs, insurance, fuel, and other life-cycle costs.

Why should contractors care about acquisition planning and life-cycle cost?

By understanding the government's responsibilities for acquisition planning and consideration of life-cycle cost, you can form persuasive arguments that help you sell more to the government. By incorporating these concepts into your proposal, or response to requests for information, or sales pitch, you can gain the trust and confidence of your government clients.

When should the process of acquisition planning begin?

Acquisition planning should begin as soon as the agency need is identified. If your company wants to influence the acquisition planning, you need to act quickly and anticipate the government's needs.

What is consolidation?

Consolidation refers to when the government combines two or more requirements into a single contract. In other words, instead of awarding two or more contracts, the government awards only one contract. Consolidation of contracts can save time and money but can also prevent smaller companies from competing on the consolidated contract. Larger contracts provide a distinct advantage for larger companies.

What is bundling?

Bundling is a minority subset of consolidation. Not all consolidation qualifies as bundling, but all bundling is also consolidation. Bundling occurs when the government consolidates two or more requirements that were previously performed by small businesses, and that consolidated contract is no longer suitable for performance by small businesses. Therefore, bundling is a subset of consolidation that shuts out the possibility of small business performing as the prime contractor. For these reasons, the government avoids bundling requirements. When the government decides to bundle contracts, they must justify the decision in writing.

Why should contractors care about government policy about consolidation and bundling?

Government contracting officers and other senior leadership are supposed to make decisions based on *market research,* including decisions about acquisition planning. Your company is part of the wider market; therefore, the opinions, arguments, or facts specific to your company qualify as market research. Your company can influence government decisions by providing information that qualifies as market research. Provide your information in writing.

You can respond to *Requests For Information (RFI)* or formal notices of consolidated or bundled contract competitions. Your written response can identify the negative impacts on small businesses, which may persuade the government to avoid consolidation or bundling. In some cases, you could write an email to the agency's Director of Small Business (or Office of Small and Disadvantaged Business Utilization or Office of Small Business Programs). The Director of Small Business may act as your company's advocate to the program or contracting office.

What is the policy on having federal employees versus contractors perform services?

That question is difficult to answer because policy preferences change every few years. So, let's discuss the decision factors so you can better understand the landscape.

What is an inherently governmental function?

An *inherently government function* is a service, action, determination, or duty so intimately related to the public interest that it requires a federal employee's performance (rather than a contractor's). Some activities cannot or should not be outsourced to contractors, we call them inherently governmental functions.

The simplest example is the President of the United States, whom Americans elect via the electoral college to be the chief executive. Although the following example is silly, it colorfully illustrates the principle of inherently governmental activities.

If the duly elected President of the United States hired a contractor to make every single decision, while the President drank margaritas in the Florida Keys, most Americans would be rightfully angry. Why is the President outsourcing the principal duties of the Office of the Presidency? Why is a contractor—who was not elected—making decisions that affect the entire nation? Why is a contractor writing and signing executive orders and negotiating deals with foreign leaders? Keep this silly example in the back of your mind when you consider other examples of inherently governmental activities.

What are some examples of inherently governmental activities?

FAR Part 7 provides a long list of inherently government activities, such as:

Conducting criminal investigations
Commanding military forces
Determining agency policy
Directing federal employees
Controlling intelligence operations
Awarding, administering, or terminating contracts
Determining agency budgets

What are some examples of functions that do not qualify as inherently governmental activities, but are awfully close to qualifying, and therefore require further scrutiny?

FAR Part 7 provides a list of functions that *almost* qualify as inherently government activities and therefore merit special consideration, including contractor services relating to the following:

Budget preparation
Reorganization or planning
Analysis, feasibility studies, and strategy options
Development of regulations
Acquisition planning
Contract management (government contracting)
Responses to Freedom of Information Act requests
Legal advice and interpretations of regulations or laws

Wait! The previous list sounds like many of the services provided by federal contractors to several different agencies. What is the explanation?

Remember, the list is a warning, not a direct prohibition. Contractors can perform services related to those functions, but the government must exercise caution to ensure the services do not cross the line of inherently governmental functions.

How does this work in the real world?

The simplest explanation is that contractors, in the 21st century, are an integral part of the federal workforce. Contractors are not federal employees, but contractors work side-by-side in support of federal employees.

While only federal employees can make decisions or determinations, contractors are regularly hired to *assist* and *support* federal employees. This difference is subtle yet important. As long as the federal employee makes the final decision or determination, contractors can usually avoid any problems with performing inherently governmental functions.

Onsite contractors should learn this word and use it often: "recommendation." As in, "My recommendation is that the agency follows simplified acquisition procedures." "I recommend that the Director conduct a full audit." "I do not recommend that the Deputy Assistant Secretary attend the meeting."

Always remember that your contractor employees, if they work as onsite contractors, side-by-side federal employees, are hired to make recommendations, *not decisions*. Let the federal employees make final decisions and determinations. Stay in your lane!

Train your employees about the policies surrounding inherently governmental functions. Each of your employees should understand the basics and know how to proceed if asked to perform inappropriate services.

FAR Part 8, Required Sources of Supplies and Services

FAR Part 8 explains the rules for placing orders against GSA Schedule contracts and directs the government to consider certain internal sources before issuing contracts.

What is the GSA Schedules Program and what is its purpose?

The General Services Administration (GSA) administers a wide variety of federal contracts for commercial supplies and services. Any federal agency can place orders against these large, *indefinite-delivery, indefinite-quantity (IDIQ) contracts.*

The paramount idea behind the GSA Schedules Program is for agencies to save time and money by ordering goods and services with pre-negotiated terms and conditions and with prices associated with bulk-buyer discounts. GSA performs all the upfront work and every agency reaps the benefits — along with the taxpayer.

What is an indefinite-delivery, indefinite-quantity contract?

An *indefinite-delivery, indefinite-quantity* or *IDIQ contract* allows agencies the flexibility to place orders for amounts they need when the need arises. If the agency knew it needed 1,000 computers in 30 days, the agency could sign a simple purchase order for 1,000 computers. This purchase order would have a definite quantity (1,000) and a definite delivery schedule (within the next 30 days).

But what if the agency knows it needs between 1,000 and 1,000,000 computers at various points within the next 5 years? Enter the IDIQ contract, which establishes a minimum and maximum quantity (between 1,000 and 1,000,000) and an ordering period (today through the next 5 years). Through this IDIQ contract, the agency can easily satisfy its needs for computers whenever they arise. Next month, the agency can order 2,000 computers. The following month, the agency can place zero orders. At the end of next year, the agency can order 30,000 computers. This flexibility is very convenient for the agency and the contracting office.

What is an order for supplies called?

A delivery order is for supplies. Sometimes a *delivery order* is abbreviated as "DO."

What is an order for services called?

A task order is for services. Sometimes a *task order* is abbreviated as "TO."

What is an ordering activity?

The *ordering activity* is the federal agency (or office) that places the order.

What is the requiring activity?

The *requiring activity* is the federal agency (or office) that needs the supplies or services.

Is the ordering activity always the same as the requiring activity?

No, sometimes the ordering activity is different from the requiring activity. For example, the Washington Headquarters Services has a contracting office that performs contracting on behalf of several other Department of Defense agencies. For example, the Office of the Secretary of Defense needs something, so it is the requiring activity. Washington Headquarters Services places the order, so it is the ordering activity.

What are the various names for the GSA Schedule contracts?

GSA Schedule contracts are also called *Federal Supply Schedule (FSS) contracts* or *Multiple Award Schedule (MAS) contracts*.

Are GSA Schedule contracts and pricing available to the public?

Yes, you can examine GSA Schedule contracts and pricing on the Internet. GSA maintains a website called *GSA Advantage* and publishes the "Authorized Federal Supply Schedule Pricelist." The GSA Advantage website also contains the *GSA E-Library*, which lists plenty of information about the GSA Schedule contract-holders. Your company can and should use this free resource to perform market research, evaluate your competitors, and gather open-source intelligence.

What is the GSA CALC Tool?

GSA also maintains a website called the *GSA CALC Tool*. CALC stands for Contract-Awarded Labor Category. The CALC Tool lets you search for actual, historical, awarded prices for orders against the various GSA Schedule contracts.

You can search by labor category and filter by education level, hourly rate, years of experience, and other factors. The CALC Tool will return the average, median, and ranges of prices (within a few standard deviations) for whatever labor category using real, historical pricing data. This CALC Tool is invaluable for your market research on the competitive labor rates for services available to the federal government. Use it! Bookmark it among your favorite websites!

What is GSA Advantage?

GSA Advantage is an online shopping service (website) for agencies to place orders against GSA Schedule contracts. Think of GSA Advantage as the central marketplace for GSA Schedule contract-holders to sell to the federal government. The government contracting officers peruse the GSA Advantage website to "shop around" and place orders against the GSA Schedule contracts.

What is GSA E-Buy?

E-Buy, E-Buy, E-Buy...Hmm, what does that sound like? The federal government is in no danger of being successfully sued for trademark infringement by E-Bay, which is a different online commerce website. Let's get back to GSA E-Buy.

GSA E-Buy is an online tool within GSA Advantage. In GSA E-Buy, agencies can publicize requirements, request price quotes, and issue orders electronically. Think of GSA E-Buy as the "online shopping center" and "checkout counter" within GSA Advantage.

Does my company need a GSA Schedule contract to be competitive?

Maybe, maybe not—it depends! Be careful with consultants who tell you that you *need* a GSA Schedule contract. For some companies, it is unnecessary and wastes time and money. For other companies, it makes business sense to obtain one or more GSA Schedule contracts.

The answer depends on what your agency sells and how your federal clients buy it. Keep in mind that only commercial products and commercial services are available on the GSA Schedule. If your company specializes in customized weaponry for the Department of Defense, you probably do not need a GSA Schedule contract (because you cannot sell noncommercial weaponry using a GSA Schedule contract). Even if your company specializes in commercial products or commercial services, maybe your top five federal clients rarely use the GSA Schedule. You need to perform market research to determine whether seeking a GSA Schedule contract will be profitable. Again, beware consultants who tell you that you *need* a GSA Schedule contract—especially if their business specializes in getting paid to hold your hand while you apply for a GSA Schedule contract!

Is every contractor that holds a GSA Schedule contract successful?

No, absolutely not! While GSA periodically "clears out the dead wood," you must understand that many GSA Schedule contract-holders are pathetically unsuccessful, with zero or very few orders. Just because you win a GSA Schedule contract does not mean your company will win any orders. You could spend tens of thousands of dollars and waste months or years applying for several GSA Schedule contracts — all for nothing!

Repeat it with me, one more time: *Just because you win a GSA Schedule contract does not mean your company will win any orders.* Think of a GSA Schedule contract like a hunting license. Just because you get the deer tags does not mean you bag the buck! So, a third time for good measure: Be careful with consultants who tell you that you *need* a GSA Schedule contract. Back away, slowly, and clutch your wallet.

If my company receives an order against my GSA Schedule contract, what terms apply to the order?

The terms and conditions of your underlying GSA Schedule contract apply to each and every order. Just because you do not see a particular clause in the order does not mean you are "off the hook." When performing a GSA order, your company is obligated to follow every clause, term, and condition found in the GSA Schedule contract.

How can my company be required to perform something that is not found in the GSA order itself?

Every GSA order is placed against a GSA Schedule contract. Every GSA order is subject to the same clauses, terms, and conditions found in the underlying GSA Schedule contract. In fact, this arrangement is one reason why the GSA Schedule system is convenient for the government. By negotiating the terms one time — in the underlying GSA Schedule contract — the government saves time and trouble when it places orders.

Are the prices in my GSA Schedule contract "set" or can they be negotiated?

Expect negotiations for every order. The prices in your GSA Schedule contract are *ceiling prices*.

What does "ceiling prices" mean?

Ceiling prices means the government will never pay a higher price than you negotiated for your GSA Schedule contract. However, the government will probably try to pay a lower price than your GSA Schedule contract rates.

Why does the government ask my company for lower prices than negotiated on my GSA Schedule contract?

The government contracting officer is following policy found in the FAR or the agency supplemental policy. Contracting officers are encouraged, if not mandated, to *try* to get a lower price than listed in the GSA Schedule contract. Remember, your GSA Schedule contract contains *ceiling prices*. The government is always free to ask for a discount from your published GSA Schedule contract rates, and they often will.

My friend told me about his troubles while negotiating the "most favored customer" pricing with the GSA contracting officer — what's up with that?

You will hear many war stories (or horror stories) about negotiating the ceiling prices on a GSA Schedule contract. The GSA contracting officer is supposed to negotiate the GSA Schedule contract pricing to achieve rates *equal to or better than* your company's "most favored customer" pricing *under similar circumstances*.

For example, your company normally sells computer laptops for $500 each. Your biggest customer, XYZ Corporation, purchased 100,000 computer laptops. This giant order made XYZ Corporation your "most favored customer" and you provided a steep discount due to the bulk volume. Only because XYZ Corporation was buying 100,000 computer laptops, you cut the price per laptop down to $300. Be careful if the GSA contracting officer negotiating your GSA Schedule contract pricing wants the price of $300 per computer laptop.

Isn't $300 per laptop my company's "most favored customer" pricing?

Yes, but you forgot the most important phrase: *under similar circumstances*. Will each of your GSA orders be for 100,000 *or more* computer laptops? Probably not. Therefore, it would be unfair (and extremely unprofitable) for your company to lock itself into a GSA Schedule contract *ceiling price* of $300 per computer laptop. What if you get nothing but orders for a single computer laptop, over and over, each for only $300 *or less*? At that rate, your company may go bankrupt.

What is the underlying lesson in this cautionary tale?

Never forget the most important phrase: *under similar circumstances*. The contracting officer negotiating your GSA Schedule contract ceiling prices is supposed to get rates that are equal to or better than your company's "most favored customer" *under similar circumstances*. Do not be shy about reminding the contracting officer that the discounted price of $300 per computer laptop was for a gigantic order of 100,000 laptops—the steepest discount your company ever offered. You can honor the same price discount with your GSA Schedule contract, *but make sure you stipulate that price applies only to GSA delivery orders for 100,000 or more laptops!* If you follow my advice, you can avoid becoming another horror story.

FAR Part 9, Contractor Qualifications

FAR Part 9 explains how federal contractors qualify for contracts by the contracting officer's determination of "responsibility."

What is a responsibility determination?

To issue your company a contract, the government must determine that your company is *responsible*. This decision about your company's "responsibility" is called a *responsibility determination*.

What federal employee performs the responsibility determination?

Government contracting officers perform responsibility determinations. Sometimes, the contracting officer will conduct a thorough review of your company to determine your responsibility. However, in most cases, the contracting officer simply checks your company's status in the *System for Award Management (SAM)* registration website for federal contractors. If nothing bad shows up, your company is assumed to be responsible.

Whenever a contracting officer signs a government contract, the signature by the contracting officer acts as a (positive, acceptable) responsibility determination. If the contracting officer signs your contract, the contracting officer effectively determines that your company is responsible.

How does the government contracting officer decide if a company is responsible?

Contracting officers use the following factors to determine whether your company is responsible and therefore eligible for federal contracts:

Does your company have adequate financial resources — or the ability to get them?
Is your company able to comply with the delivery or performance schedule?

Does your company have a satisfactory record of past performance?
Does your company have a history of integrity and business ethics?
Does your company have the organizational and operational controls to succeed?
Does your company have the accounting and technical skills to succeed?
Does your company have the necessary production, construction, or technical equipment or facilities to succeed?

This previous list of factors seems vague, arbitrary, and subjective. How can my company predict if it will be judged as responsible or not?

Do not overthink this topic. The government wants the ability to say "no" to risky contractors. Think of the responsibility determination as the government "kicking the tires" to make sure the contractor is on the up-and-up and can perform the contract successfully.

Do subcontractors need to be determined responsible?

Yes, as a prime contractor, it is your company's duty to ensure that any subcontractors you engage to perform the contract are also responsible. Just as the government can "kick the tires" of your company as the prime contractor, your company needs to take a closer look at any subcontractors. Your company should carefully evaluate any potential subcontractors that may perform work on your federal prime contracts. Remember, if the subcontractor fails or causes problems, those problems are entirely *your problem* as the prime contractor.

What are the databases the government checks to determine the responsibility of my company?

The government is supposed to check the status of your company in the *System for Award Management (SAM)*. (When SAM was being upgraded and integrated with other systems, the government temporarily called it Beta.SAM.)

The government may also check the *Federal Awardee Performance and Integrity Information System (FAPIIS)* and the *Contractor Performance Assessment Reporting System (CPARS)*.

What is CPARS?

CPARS is incredibly important for the success (or failure!) of your company in government contracting. Every federal contract above a certain dollar threshold requires the contracting officer to record an assessment of the performance of your company into CPARS. Therefore, CPARS is an online database of past performance of federal contractors.

Other contracting officers and other federal agencies will look up the past performance evaluations of your company within CPARS. If you have negative evaluations or disagreeable information in CPARS, other federal clients will see it and will avoid your company like the plague.

Can my company monitor what the government records in CPARS?

Yes, and your company should carefully monitor any CPARS action. Find out the timelines for when your government client will enter information into CPARS. Immediately read and analyze the information about your company in CPARS, which will be made available to you. If you find negative information, do your best to rebut or respond to the negative information. If you are persistent and lucky, maybe you can convince the government to change or remove your negative commentary and other information.

Are you saying it is difficult and unlikely for my company to change the negative information entered into CPARS?

Yes, it is difficult and unlikely for your company to succeed in changing CPARS information. CPARS is a tool designed, created, and maintained for the government's benefit, so the government wants its employees to have broad discretion to be honest and candid about CPARS evaluations.

What can my company do about negative CPARS information?

Your company has the right to respond, in writing, to the CPARS evaluation. Make sure you respond before the deadline. Commit significant resources to your formal response, as if the future of your company depends on it—because it does!

How should my company write its response to negative CPARS information?

Your response to negative CPARS information must be objective, professional, and detailed. You must include dates, references to the contract, and specific events or facts. Never include personal insults, personal attacks, or insinuations about the conduct of federal employees. Instead, focus on what your company did along with the facts of when, why, and how. Match your company's actions to the contractual requirements. Quote the contract if necessary. Stay objective!

How can my company prepare for a strong CPARS response or rebuttal?

Preparation is the key to a persuasive rebuttal or response to negative CPARS evaluations. Your company wins or loses this contest months and years before you submit your response into CPARS.

During the performance of any federal contract or subcontract, documentation is your best friend. Save everything. Document everything. Get in the habit of writing yourself and others in your company emails and memoranda for the record.

Phone calls never happened unless you document the substance of the phone call in an email or memorandum. In-person conversations never happened unless you document it afterwards. Are you detecting a pattern? Your company needs to develop a complete "paper trail" (or "email trail").

FAR Part 10, Market Research

FAR Part 10 directs the government to perform market research to make better contracting decisions. Savvy contractors influence the process of market research.

Why does the government conduct market research?

The government conducts *market research* to make decisions about the contracting process. Should every company be eligible to compete? Should this contract be set aside for small businesses or for women-owned small businesses? Is there a commercial product available or should the government pay someone to develop something new?

The fruits of market research may answer some or all these questions. Whether the government consolidates it into a formal market research report or not, the process of collecting and analyzing market research is designed to *influence future government contracts.* Are you paying attention?

Who conducts market research for a competitive government contract?

Although the contracting officer is ultimately response for performing market research, other federal employees may help. The program office which needs the goods or services may assist in performing market research.

What will the government explore to conduct market research?

Anything within reason. The government can examine prior contracts, search the Internet, attend conferences, invite potential contractors to an "industry day" at the agency, or pick up the phone and call people. Maybe the government will read trade journals, scientific articles, or attend training to learn more about a specific industry or technology. Maybe the government will email your company with a series of questions. Answer that email!

Is market research by the government an open-ended task with many possible methods?

Yes, I'm glad you picked up on that characteristic. Market research can be almost anything if it gives the government useful information to make a contracting decision.

When should the government's market research process begin?

Market research should begin as soon as the federal agency identifies a need (realizes it wants to buy something).

When should the government's market research process end?

The government uses its best judgment to determine how much market research is optimal or necessary. Depending on the size, complexity, urgency, dollar value, or other factors, market research could take ten minutes or ten months or more.

How can contractors influence the market research process?

Market research is your opportunity to be heard. The government collects market research to make decisions. If you provide the market research, you influence the decisions. If you do not provide any information for the government's market research, you have ceded the opportunity to your competitors.

Therefore, tell the government why you deserve the contract. Are you the best? Fastest? Lowest priced (but are you technically acceptable)? What's your special set-aside signal? Are you a small business? Women-owned small business or WOSB? Let the government know. Explain why your type of business is the only type of business that should qualify.

Even if you are a large business, you can persuade the government that small businesses do not have the capacity, connections, or scale. Now is your chance to make sure the level of competition favors your unique classifications, whether you're a small business or a large conglomerate.

What is a Request for Information or RFI?

A *Request for Information (RFI)* is an open invitation — from the government to any company — to provide the government with "market research." Again, you should seize this opportunity. Your company has the chance to create and influence the government's market research report. Inform the government about your company's capabilities.

Releasing the RFI simply means the government is curious. There may or may not be an actual requirement for an upcoming contract. The government is asking for information to shape the decision and potential contract. For example, the government releases a RFI to determine the current level of technology in 3-D printing or what automated accounting services are available.

Should my company respond to the RFI to influence future government contracts?

Yes, always respond to a relevant RFI. You can influence the future contract in a way that helps you win. This is your opportunity to explain why your technology or capability is exactly the solution the government needs. You can gain a significant advantage over your competitors by responding to the RFI. By explaining the benefits of your products or services, you can nudge the government requirements down a path that leads straight to your company.

What is a Sources Sought Notice?

Sources Sought Notice or *SSN* means the government wants to know what types of businesses will compete for an upcoming contract. Think of the SSN as a special type of RFI. Instead of general information like the RFI requests, the SSN explores what businesses exist, what products and services they offer, and most importantly, how these businesses are classified for potential contract set-asides.

Government contracts can be "set aside" for specific types of businesses, like small businesses or women-owned small businesses. Read Part 6, Competition Requirements, and Part 19, Small Business Programs for more information.

Can my response to the RFI or SSN create a small business set-aside?

Yes, if several small businesses reply to the SSN, then the government may set aside the contract so that only small businesses can compete. If many women-owned small businesses reply, maybe the contract will be a women-owned small business set-aside.

Always respond to a relevant SSN for the same reason that you should always respond to a relevant RFI. You can influence the future contract by eliminating your competitors who do not share your status as a small business or another socioeconomic classification.

If enough businesses in the same socioeconomic classification respond to the SSN, they can "corner the market" for themselves and exclude everyone else. Conversely, even large businesses should respond so that the government knows that large businesses are interested and can satisfy the requirements. Think of the SSN or RFI as a battle to determine whether the government contract will be set aside. Join the fight!

FAR Part 11, Describing Agency Needs

FAR Part 11 explains how the government describes what it wants to buy.

What is the government's policy for describing what it wants to buy?

The government has several policy goals when describing what it wants to buy from industry, including:

Using market research to formulate an intelligent description of what it wants
Promoting full and open competition
Using restrictive conditions only as necessary
Encouraging commercial supplies or services
Describing requirements in terms of functions to be provided, performance specifications, or essential physical characteristics

What does it mean to describe requirements in terms of functions to provide, performance specifications, or essential physical characteristics?

The goal of these policies is to shape government solicitations towards objective outcomes or characteristics so that any qualified contractor can win and perform the contract. Avoid using a brand name or proprietary technology in the description of the requirement so that many companies can compete, instead of just one or few.

For example, let's discuss the agency's need for laptop computers. We will start with a very poor, anticompetitive description of the agency's needs:

> "The agency needs an Apple-branded laptop computer that has smooth edges."

This description is anticompetitive because only Apple can manufacture the laptop. There are no required functions or performance specifications. Also, having smooth edges sounds like a personal preference, not an essential physical characteristic that will help the agency or its employees.

Let's modify the agency's description to fit the policy goals found in FAR Part 11:

> "The agency needs a laptop computer that contains a disk drive, performs with no interruption in very hot weather (above 90 degrees Fahrenheit), and can fit within a backpack that is 16 inches wide, 20 inches long, and 8 inches deep."

Now the requirements follow the policy goals of FAR Part 11 by describing objective performance specifications, functions, or physical characteristics.

Disk drive (function to be provided)
Performs in hot weather (performance specification)
Fits in a backpack (essential physical characteristic)

What is the common theme shared between performance specifications, required functions, and essential physical characteristics?

The common theme is these factors are objective needs (rather than subjective preferences) and can be satisfied by almost any company, rather than a single company. These factors are not proprietary or monopolized by a single brand or company. Any company can evaluate these objective characteristics to determine whether they can provide the item. As such, the revised statement of what the government needs will attract more companies and proposals and therefore, more competition.

Why does the government prefer commercial, rather than custom, solutions?

Commercial solutions are available immediately and have been sold (or offered) to the open market—not just to the government. Developing a new product or new service includes, of course, development and testing costs. The custom-developed item may not work as reliably as solutions that go back many years. Finally, the custom-developed item will usually have a price higher than a commercial solution because the custom item has only one potential customer—the government.

Does the government buy commercial items using a different method of contracting?

Yes, the federal government has commercial procedures for procuring commercial items. These commercial procedures significantly speed up the government contracting process. Therefore, commercial procedures are preferred by law and regulation. Remind the government of the preference for commercial items and commercial procedures whenever possible. For more information, read Part 12, Acquisition of Commercial Items.

Does the term "commercial items" include goods and services?

Yes, the term *commercial items* include products and services. Your company's products and your company's services may be classified as "commercial items" for government contracting purposes. Remember: Commercial items include both physical goods and intangible services.

Can the government restrict the contract competition to a particular brand name?

Yes, some government contract solicitations will restrict competition to a particular brand name. Other competitions will restrict competition to *brand name or equal*, which allows a contractor to provide a comparable substitute.

What rules must the government follow to restrict the solicitation to a brand name?

If the solicitation is restricted to a particular *brand name only*, the government must say so explicitly and explain its justification. It is acceptable to limit competition to a brand name, but there must be a reason the government needs the brand name. It cannot be based solely on a brand preference. There must be some other relevant or "salient" characteristic of the brand name that benefits the government.

Requiring Apple products is an example of a government contract competition restricted to a brand name. The justification could be that the entire information technology system of the government is compatible only with Apple products. However, the justification cannot be that the government employees simply "like" Apple products.

Why would the government restrict the solicitation to brand name or equal?

Brand name or equal allows slightly broader competition than a solicitation limited to a specific brand name. If the government knows that the objective specifications of a brand-name product will meet the requirement, reliance on brand name or equal could make sense. Whenever possible, the government should restrict to *brand name or equal* rather than *brand name only*.

The government does not need the specific brand, but it knows that the *performance characteristics* of a particular brand will satisfy its needs. If there is some other brand or manufacturer that can provide at least the same objective specifications, the government will have no problem contracting with the alternative brand or manufacturer.

For example, the government could restrict competition to something *brand name or equal* to the Apple iPhone X. The government could list the objective specifications of the Apple iPhone X, which the contractor must meet or exceed to win the contract. Apple can win this competition by supplying the iPhone X. However, any Apple competitor can also win this competition if it supplies a cell phone that meets or exceeds the same specifications. In this way, *brand name or equal* provides more competition, more options, and therefore better pricing than restricting to *brand name only*.

Is a brand name restriction the same as a sole-source contract?

A *sole-source government contract* means that one company alone on planet Earth can provide the goods or services. The government must write, sign, and publicize a special justification to restrict competition to only one source. Read more about this special justification in Part 6, Competition Requirements.

Sole source is not the same as *brand name only*. For example, Honda cars can be sold by many different car dealerships. Many Honda dealerships are not owned by Honda. In contrast, Tesla cars are sold by authorized Tesla dealerships only. No Tesla resellers currently exist (in this example). If the government requires a Honda brand name, many sources exist to deliver the Honda brand name, *i.e.*, Honda dealerships. In contrast, if the government requires a Tesla brand name, this requirement is effectively "sole source" because only Tesla can supply the car.

FAR Part 12, Acquisition of Commercial Items

FAR Part 12 provides streamlined procedures for buying commercial items and encourages the purchase of commercial items whenever possible.

Why does the government prefer commercial solutions rather than custom solutions?

Commercial solutions are available immediately and have been sold (or offered) to the open market—not just to the government. Developing a new product or new service includes, of course, development and testing costs. The custom-developed item may not work as reliably as solutions that have existed for many years. Finally, the custom-developed item will usually have a higher price than a commercial solution because the custom item has only one potential customer—the government.

What is the paramount goal of the special procedures for contracting for commercial items?

Copy the private sector to save time and money. Mirror, match, and mimic as many customary terms and conditions as possible. Streamline or eliminate as many FAR clauses or mandatory procedures as possible. Doesn't that sound reasonable?

How can you call them "commercial contracting procedures" if the result is a government contract?

Do not spend too much time worrying about the contradiction in terms. Let me explain. While a contract negotiated using the commercial procedures of FAR Part 12 is a government contract, it is a special type of government contract.

The commercial procedures in FAR Part 12 are designed to mimic private-sector, commercial standards as much as possible. Although it will not be the same as a private-sector, nongovernment contract, a FAR Part 12 contract will be a "middle ground" that is preferable to a traditionally negotiated government contract. Do not let the perfect be the enemy of the good. Understand that the commercial procedures of FAR Part 12 are designed to transform the government contracting process as much as possible into the more efficient and familiar process known in the private sector.

Should a contractor prefer to win and perform a commercial contract using FAR Part 12 procedures?

Yes, if your company gets a choice between a traditional government contract and a streamlined, commercial contract using FAR Part 12 procedures, the decision is simple. Your company prefers the FAR Part 12 contract in almost any imaginable circumstance.

Why does the government prefer using the commercial contracting procedures of FAR Part 12?

The commercial contracting procedures of FAR Part 12 allow for a faster, streamlined, more convenient method than using more "traditional" government contracting procedures.

Why are the commercial contracting procedures of FAR Part 12 faster, streamlined, and more convenient?

The commercial procedures of FAR Part 12 are streamlined because they remove many of the FAR clauses required in other, noncommercial government contracts. The difference in the number of FAR clauses in a traditional government contract versus a FAR Part 12 contract should be striking. Further, the commercial procedures of FAR Part 12 allow the government to skip or minimize several of the procedural steps required in other types of government contract competitions.

The commercial procedures of FAR Part 12 are convenient for your company because they encourage adopting the standards, terms, or practices that already exist in the private sector. Your company may be accustomed to standard commercial practices. Rather than having to adopt your company practices to the government standards, the government is supposed to accommodate the customary practices of the private sector. All these benefits of FAR Part 12 mean that commercial contracts are usually solicited, negotiated, and awarded much faster than traditional government contracts.

Can my company suggest that the government should use FAR Part 12 procedures?

Yes, whenever appropriate, your company can and should suggest using the commercial procedures of FAR Part 12. Explain how these commercial procedures can save time and money by streamlining the process.

When is it appropriate for my company to suggest, and for the government to use, the commercial procedures of FAR Part 12?

Whenever the government wants to buy a product or service that can be classified as commercial, you should be using commercial procedures under FAR Part 12.

Who determines whether the item (product or service) qualifies as commercial?

The contracting officer has the final say in determining whether a product or service qualifies as a "commercial item." By writing a *determination and findings (D&F)* or *commerciality determination memo*, the contracting officer makes the final decision.

If commercial procedures are so convenient, why would a contracting officer deny that a product or service qualifies as a commercial item?

One potential reason is that the contracting officer wants to force your company to submit certified cost or pricing data. Qualification as a commercial item is a specific exemption to the requirement to provide certified cost or pricing data. Read more about certified cost or pricing data in Part 15, Contracting by Negotiation.

Who determines whether the contract itself will use commercial procedures?

Again, the contracting officer chooses to use commercial procedures or otherwise. Convince the contracting officer to use commercial procedures because they are faster, cheaper, easier, and preferred by law and regulation.

When using commercial procedures under FAR Part 12, can my company ask the government to accommodate standard commercial terms and conditions?

Yes, and this fact is one of the most important benefits of using commercial procedures. When you are lucky enough to be using commercial procedures, ask the government to match, mirror, or mimic your company's terms and conditions from the private sector. The government should accommodate reasonable commercial procedures. Why reinvent the wheel?

For example, if your company's standard terms and conditions directly contradict the "commercial" contract you're about to sign, negotiate a change to the contract. If your usual delivery schedule differs from the government's request, ask for an accommodation. Anything can and should be negotiated; you just need to ask. Remind the contracting officer of the preference for adopting commercial practices—including terms and conditions—when using the commercial procedures of FAR Part 12.

Will my commercial contract include the dangerous Changes clause?

No, it should not include the dangerous Changes clause. (Read more about the Changes clause in Part 43, Contract Modifications.) Commercial contracts should instead require any changes to be mutually agreed upon in writing rather than the unilateral process allowed by the Changes clause. Do not sign a contract that is supposed to be commercial under FAR Part 12 procedures yet includes a version of the Changes clause.

What is the most common form the government uses for commercial contracts?

You should expect to see a *SF 1449* or *Standard Form 1449*, which the government often uses for the contract you sign.

What are the two FAR clauses that indicate my contract uses the commercial procedures of FAR Part 12?

The obvious sign of a commercial contract using FAR Part 12 procedures is this pair of clauses:

FAR 52.212-4
FAR 52.212-5

If you cannot find both clauses in your allegedly commercial contract, ask the contracting officer. Something may be very, very wrong...

Can my company be subject to Cost Accounting Standards under a commercial contract?

No, the general rule is that Cost Accounting Standards (CAS) do not apply to commercial contracts. For more information about CAS, read Part 30, Cost Accounting Standards Administration and Part 31, Contract Cost Principles and Procedures.

What payment arrangement can my company expect for a commercial contract?

Most commercial contracts will use a firm-fixed-price payment structure. If the contracting officer writes a memo which justifies the decision, the commercial contract may use a labor-hours or time-and-materials payment structure. To read more about these payment arrangements, read Part 16, Types of Contracts.

FAR Part 13, Simplified Acquisition Procedures

FAR Part 13 explains the simplified acquisition procedures and their dollar thresholds.

What is the first fact you should memorize about FAR Part 13 and simplified acquisition procedures?

You should know the dollar threshold for using simplified procedures for certain commercial items, found in FAR 13.5.

Why should all contractors know this dollar threshold?

If you offer commercial products or commercial services, in an amount equal to or less than this threshold, the government can procure these items using the simplified procedures of FAR Part 13. Both government and contractor will be pleased if you can use the simplified acquisition procedures because they're faster and *simpler*.

What is the dollar threshold for using FAR 13.5 for commercial items?

Throughout this book, I strive to avoid using any dollar thresholds and specific FAR quotations because the FAR changes so often. As of writing this paragraph, the dollar threshold listed in FAR 13.5 is $7.5 million, but the threshold will change. You need to check the current threshold yourself. Again, if you provide commercial products or commercial services, in amounts within this dollar threshold found in FAR 13.5, push the government to use simplified procedures.

What if my company's products or services are not commercial?

If your company's products or services are noncommercial, the dollar threshold for using FAR Part 13 procedures is the simplified acquisition threshold or SAT. Be careful to distinguish the *simplified acquisition threshold (SAT)* from the threshold for using simplified procedures for commercial items. The names of these different thresholds are confusingly similar, so pay attention.

What is the second fact you should memorize about FAR Part 13 and simplified acquisition procedures?

The second fact you should memorize is the simplified acquisition threshold or SAT.

What is the simplified acquisition threshold?

Again, I want to avoid quoting dollar thresholds because such amounts change often. As of writing this paragraph, the simplified acquisition threshold (defined in FAR Part 2, Definitions of Words and Terms) is $250,000, but the threshold will change. You need to check the current threshold yourself.

The simplified acquisition threshold (SAT) is relevant for noncommercial products and services. Anything your company provides in amounts at or below this dollar threshold (even if they are noncommercial) can be procured using simplified procedures.

What is one more reason to memorize the simplified acquisition threshold?

Any government contract at or below the simplified acquisition threshold is—*by default*—reserved exclusively for small businesses. The government must "rebut the presumption" (provide good reason) for not using a small business set-aside within the simplified acquisition threshold. The Small Business Administration closely tracks each agency's adherence to this special rule favoring small businesses.

What is the government's documentation burden when using simplified acquisition procedures?

The stated policy of the government is to keep documentation to a minimum when using simplified acquisition procedures under FAR Part 13. Therefore, simplified acquisition procedures require sparse documentation, especially when compared to other methods of government contracting.

What is the government's competition standard when using simplified acquisition procedures?

When using simplified acquisition procedures, the government must promote competition to the "maximum extent practicable." This competition standard is significantly less stringent than the "full and open competition" required under FAR Part 15 (Contracting by Negotiation) or other procedures.

Why did Congress create the simplified acquisition procedures?

Simplified acquisitions are designed to be simple. Congress created simplified acquisitions as a specific "carve-out" or exemption from full and open competition. Recognizing that full and open competition often takes longer and ends up in litigation or protests, Congress purposefully relaxed the competitive standard and the procurement rules to create the simplified acquisition procedures.

What makes the simplified acquisition procedures so simple?

Many of the benefits of simplified acquisition procedures are because of what is *not* required. Simplified acquisitions relax or omit several onerous rules. While complex source selections under FAR Part 15 require the following, simplified acquisition procedures do not require:

Establishment of a competitive range
Formal evaluation plans
Formal discussions with each company in the competitive range
Strict adherence to deadlines for receipt of proposals
Extensive documentation of the evaluation and negotiation process
Notification of unsuccessful companies
Formal debriefings of unsuccessful companies
Evaluation factors stated in terms of their relative importance to each other

Using simplified acquisition procedures, the government can skip everything in the list. The complicated procedures of FAR Part 14 and FAR Part 15 are expressly exempted from FAR Part 13. The lack of rigorous procedures in FAR Part 13 leaves ample room for interpretation. Contracting officers are encouraged to use "innovative approaches" when awarding contracts using simplified acquisition procedures.

Is a price quotation the same as submitting an offer to the government?

No! *A quotation is not an offer*, despite how people mix up the two. There is an important contractual distinction between a quotation (a price quote) and an offer in government contracting. A valid contract needs an offer, an acceptance, and consideration (exchange of value). Let's consider formal proposals before we return to mere price quotes.

Is my proposal an offer to the government?

Yes, your *proposal is an offer* the government can accept by issuing you a contract. The government has the power to accept or reject your offer, which appears in the form of a proposal.

If my company responds to a formal Request for Proposals, is the response an offer?

Yes, when you submit a full proposal in response to a *Request for Proposals (RFP)*, your proposal is an offer to the government. You offer your services, product, or solution. You ask for a contract. The government can accept or reject your proposal (which is your offer).

How does the government accept my proposal (offer)?

The government accepts your proposal (offer) by issuing you a contract. With proposals in response to a RFP, the government has the power to accept or reject any offer. The government has the "last word" in whether there will be a contract or not. You made the initial offer with your proposal, but the government is free to accept or reject it.

For these reasons, should my company always include an expiration date on formal proposals?

Yes, since your proposal is an offer, you should always include an expiration date on your proposal. You do not want to keep your offer open forever, or for an extended period of time.

Think about how long your proposal offer should last and set a limit. Write a proviso something like "This proposal expires on August 21" or "The terms of this proposal remain in effect for ninety (90) days after submission and receipt by the government." However, be careful to comply with any minimum amount of time your offer must remain open if it is required by the government in the RFP. Now, let's return to price quotes.

If my price quote is not an offer, then what is it?

Think of your quote as a detail of information the government can use to decide how to purchase goods or services, but do not think of your quote as an offer. In a sense, your price quote is an element of *market research*. Learn more about market research in Part 10, Market Research.

If my company sends a price quote, can the government accept it and form a binding contract?

No. Remember, a quotation (price quote) is not an offer to the government. The government cannot accept a mere quote because there is no offer to accept. Remember, in order to form a contract, you need offer, acceptance, and consideration.

If the government cannot accept my price quote because it is not an offer, then who makes the initial offer?

The government makes the offer to your company in the form of a purchase order. The government will consider and evaluate several quotes and then choose the best one. Since your *quote is not an offer*, there is no offer for the government to accept. Therefore, the government must make the initial offer.

What common form will the government use to make an offer to my company after receiving a price quote?

Usually, the government will send your company a purchase order using the *Standard Form 1449 (SF 1449)*. If you sell commercial items to the government, you will become very familiar with SF 1449.

Is the SF 1449 an offer to my company?

Yes, the SF 1449 (purchase order) is an offer. The proof is on the front page, which will specify whether the contractor is required to sign the purchase order and return it to the government.

Are you saying my company has the power to accept or reject the purchase order?

Yes, if you sign the purchase order, you exercise your power to accept the contract.

What if the SF 1449 does not require a signature from my company?

You can accept this offer (purchase order) "by performance" rather by signature. When the SF 1449 (purchase order) does not require your signature, you accept the offer — and form a binding contract — by performing the actual contract.

If the purchase order is for supplies, when you deliver the goods, you show that you have accepted the contract. If the SF 1449 is for services, you accept the contract by performing the services.

What about the period of time after the government sends the purchase order but before the company accepts by performance?

There may be a lengthy period when the government has no idea whether you accepted the offer (purchase order, SF 1449) or not. The government either embraces that risk or eliminates the risk by requiring your signature. It is for the government to choose since the government initiated and created the offer.

What types of purchase orders may not require a signature?

If a purchase order does not require a signature, it will usually be for short-term delivery of supplies to the government. For the delivery of commercial goods that are not mission-critical, the government will sometimes forego the signature requirement. You accept such an offer (and form a contract) by sending the supplies, and the government should pay you within 30 days.

Is my company required to accept or reject a purchase order, whether by signature or performance?

No. The purchase order (SF 1449) is an offer. Sometimes it requires your signature; sometimes it does not. In either case, you are not required to accept, reject, or notify the government. You have no duty to accept or reject. You could throw the purchase order into the trash and ignore it forever.

What happens if my company ignores purchase orders?

You should not ignore purchase orders. Contempt or inattention is bad for business. Always respond promptly (whether yes or no) so that you encourage the government to give you more business. Even if your signature is not required, it is helpful to send the government an email message or to call to say that you plan to deliver or perform. The government contracting officers appreciate that gesture.

FAR Part 14, Sealed Bidding

FAR Part 14 provides procedures for using sealed bidding.

What is the history of sealed bidding?

Many years ago, public officials gathered in town halls to open sealed envelopes, in a public setting, to guarantee fairness and transparency. These *sealed bids* became the basis for contracting competition. The government notified everyone through "formal advertising" to submit a bid based on government specifications. If your bid was compliant and the lowest price, your bid wins the competition.

When Congress passed the *Competition in Contracting Act (CICA)* in 1984, the popularity of sealed bidding dropped significantly. The reason is under CICA, both sealed bidding under FAR Part 14 and competitive negotiation under FAR Part 15 were acceptable ways to satisfy the need for "full and open competition." In most cases, agencies opted to use the more flexible procedures of FAR Part 15 instead of sealed bidding.

Is sealed bidding a common practice now?

No, not really. In federal government contracting, sealed bidding is a rare or niche method of competition. Only a small minority of government contract competitions use sealed bidding. Unless you work in construction contracting, you can probably ignore it completely.

How does the government invite sealed bids?

The "solicitation" for sealed bidding is called an *Invitation for Bids* or *IFB*. To give all companies an equal opportunity, the IFB should contain all the important terms and conditions of the contract. The idea behind this policy is that bidders should distinguish themselves primarily on price.

How does the government select a winner under sealed bidding?

Price is supposed to be the primary decision factor for award. Ideally, the government shared a precise and exhaustive list of specifications so that all bidders understand exactly what must be performed under the contract. Therefore, the only evaluation factor should be price or price-related factors.

Can the government negotiate under sealed bidding?

No, the government cannot negotiate with bidders under sealed bidding. Remember, the bids are sealed, and the winner is selected based only on price evaluation. This limitation is both the strength and weakness of sealed bidding. The benefit is the sealed bidding process is objective, simple, and prevents unequal treatment of bidders. The drawback is the process is rigid, limited, and prevents negotiation that might otherwise produce a better contract deal.

Does the government have discretion to pay more for higher quality or performance under sealed bidding?

No, sealed bidding is designed to prevent the government from paying more to get a better product or service. Under sealed bidding, the government is supposed to award to the company that has a "responsive" bid with the lowest price.

What does "responsive" mean under sealed bidding?

Responsive refers to whether the bid conforms to all material elements of the IFB or government specifications. If your company leaves out an important item required by the IFB, or fails to follow the IFB, your bid may be considered *nonresponsive*. If your bid is nonresponsive, you are not eligible for award.

The requirement of responsiveness is one way to keep all sealed bidders on equal footing. If one bidder tries to get an unfair advantage by submitting a lower price based on a material deviation from the IFB, the government cannot possibly reward that bidder because such a bid is nonresponsive and therefore ineligible for award.

What is the difference between responsiveness versus responsibility?

Responsiveness is about whether the contractor pledged to do precisely what the government requested in the IFB. The government will examine only your bid to determine responsiveness to the IFB.

Responsibility is about whether the contractor can or will perform the contract (if it wins the contract). The government can examine not only your bid, but other attributes of your company as well, to determine responsibility. You can read more about the determination of contractor responsibility in Part 9, Contractor Qualifications.

What is two-step sealed bidding?

If you understand so far, sealed bidding does not allow negotiation between the government and sealed bidders. Instead, the government opens the sealed bids and makes award based only on price or price-related factors.

Two-step sealed bidding combines negotiation with traditional sealed bidding. In the first step, the government asks for different technical proposals. No pricing or price negotiation is involved in the first step. The government only negotiates regarding the technical proposal. The goal is to develop a detailed technical specification to use in the second step.

The second step is more like traditional sealed bidding. Based on the technical specification developed in the first step, companies submit sealed bids, and the government picks the winner based on the lowest price.

Why would the government use two-step sealed bidding?

Two-step sealed bidding makes sense when the government does not have a precise set of technical standards already developed, which is a requirement for traditional sealed bidding.

Two-step sealed bidding allows creative input and ideas from industry, and helps the government decide what it wants and what is available in the first step. Then, in the second step, the government takes those specifications and follows a process like traditional sealed bidding.

FAR Part 15, Contracting By Negotiation

FAR Part 15 explains the process for the most complicated source selection process and provides the rules for submitting certified cost or pricing data.

Welcome to the "big leagues" of FAR Part 15.

Why do you call FAR Part 15 the big leagues?

The largest and most complex source selections typically use FAR Part 15 procedures. If the government needs a new contract for hundreds of millions of dollars, it will likely use the source selection procedures of FAR Part 15.

What are the two "flavors" of FAR Part 15 source selections?

The two "flavors" of FAR Part 15 source selections are *tradeoff* and *lowest price, technically acceptable (LPTA)*.

What does tradeoff mean?

Tradeoff means the government can "trade off" price against nonprice evaluation factors, like past performance, experience, technical qualifications, or management planning.

Does the tradeoff method allow flexibility for the government's decision?

Yes, the government has significant flexibility in selecting the winning proposal when using the tradeoff method.

In a tradeoff, can the government award to the highest priced offeror, or to the lowest priced offeror, or to neither the highest nor lowest priced offeror?

Yes, yes, and yes.

How is it possible for the government to have so many choices during a tradeoff?

Tradeoffs are subjective. The tradeoff method balances the government's preference for a lower price against one or more nonprice evaluation factors like technical specifications or past performance. Measuring the objective benefit of paying a higher price for a higher rated, nonprice evaluation factor is difficult, if not impossible. Therefore, the government measures its comparative preference for different combinations of price and nonprice ratings by something called the "price premium."

What is the price premium?

Price premium refers to how much the government values an increase from one rating of a nonprice evaluation factor to another, higher rating of a nonprice evaluation factor. This increase usually comes with a corresponding price increase. (If one proposal was rated higher than another, but had the same price, there is no reason to select the lower rated proposal.)

For example, company XYZ submits a proposal for $100 that is rated "Excellent" for past performance. Company ABC submits a proposal for $90 that is rated "Marginal" for past performance. The price premium represents the "extra" $10 price difference that gets the government a contractor that is rated "Excellent" instead of "Marginal."

The government can decide that $10 is worth the marginal increase from "Marginal" to "Excellent." Or the government can decide that $10 is not worth the marginal increase. This decision concerns the "price premium," which will be mentioned or discussed in any detailed source selection decision document.

What is a source selection decision document?

The *source selection decision document* is a formal memo explaining the government's subjective choice of a winner in a tradeoff source selection. There are many other names for this memo, but the function remains the same: provide the government's reasoning for selecting the winning contractor's proposal instead of the unsuccessful proposals. Unless there is one proposal that is rated higher and priced lower than every single other proposal (which is unlikely), the decision document will need to account for the different "price premiums" between the competitive proposals.

Does the contracting officer make the decision on which contractor's proposal to select for award?

Often, but not always. The default rule is that the contracting officer is the *source selection authority*, or the single decisionmaker for selecting the winning contractor. However, in larger and more complex contracts, the source selection authority or SSA will be someone other than the contracting officer, such as a senior official in the agency.

Does the source selection authority read every proposal?

No, the *source selection authority (SSA)* will probably not read every proposal. Nor must the SSA evaluate every proposal, nor must the SSA read every evaluation. Instead, the SSA may receive a high-level briefing from the evaluation team (the people who actually read the proposals and provide written evaluations based on the evaluation factors). The high-level briefing will review the final evaluation ratings of the top proposals and may recommend selection of a particular contractor.

What does LPTA mean?

Lowest price, technically acceptable (LPTA) creates a race to the bottom. The government sets the minimum specifications. Any proposal that meets or exceeds the minimum specifications is eligible. Proposals that are *technically acceptable* will be ranked on price. The lowest price, technically acceptable proposal wins.

Using LPTA, can the government award to a higher priced proposal?

No, LPTA requires the government to select the proposal that is lowest priced and technically acceptable. The hands of the government are tied in this respect, with no discretion.

Using LPTA, can my company be rewarded for providing specifications or capabilities that exceed the minimum?

No, under LPTA, proposals will not receive extra credit or favored treatment for exceeding the minimum requirement. Your company should focus on price while providing no effort beyond what is required for technical acceptability.

What is the most important condition for using the LPTA selection process?

The most important condition for using LPTA is that government needs are clearly defined. If government requirements are not clearly defined, the government cannot set the bar for technical acceptability, or the minimum level for eligibility.

What is an evaluation factor?

Government contracting competitions disclose evaluation factors to let potential contractors know what is important to the clients. If price is important, price will be an evaluation factor. If past performance and technical specifications are important, those too will be evaluation factors.

Evaluation factor is a term of art in government contracting. Think of the evaluation factor as some attribute or characteristic of the potential contractor that generates a benefit to the government (or which creates a risk if it is absent or deficient).

Let's say one evaluation factor is a security mitigation plan for power outages. If a potential contractor has a thorough, logical, and time-tested security mitigation plan, that plan is a significant benefit to the government client. It may contain one or more strengths that translate into a favorable evaluation factor rating.

If a different potential contractor has a nonsensical plan, that detail is certainly a risk for the government client. This weakness can translate into a poor evaluation factor rating. In this example, these two potential contractors will be scored or evaluated differently on the evaluation factor of a security mitigation plan.

What is the most common evaluation factor for government contract competitions?

The most common evaluation factor is *price*. Unless there is a special exception, price will be evaluated for all government contract awards. Even during competitions where price is the least important factor, such as in some tradeoff competitions, price is still evaluated.

What are some other evaluation factors for government contract competitions?

Other common evaluation factors include *past performance, experience,* and *technical approach.*

What is technical approach?

Technical approach is a very broad evaluation factor that may include subfactors. Sometimes the technical approach factor is simply to evaluate exactly how the potential contractor will perform the contract. Overreliance on technical approach may indicate that this government contracting opportunity is an "essay-writing contest." In other words, how you write the proposal may be just as important as the objective content or promises within your proposal. Style and presentation may matter more than substance!

Is the government limited to using specific types of evaluation factors?

No, the government can choose any number of evaluation factors. It can always create a new evaluation factor. If you can imagine some feature or attribute of a potential contractor that matters to success under a government contract, you can imagine an evaluation factor to measure that feature or attribute.

What is past performance?

Past performance is a common way the government can evaluate your proposal or your company. Price is the single most common evaluation factor, but past performance is a likely close second or third. To reduce the risk of failure, the government wants contractors who have already "been there, done that."

Government clients know that history repeats itself. Looking to the past can help you to predict the future. The past performance of your company is so important to winning new government contracts.

Should my company keep track of all its past performance?

Yes, you should keep a detailed database of your past company performance. This database should include past performance with government clients and other, private sector businesses. Keep track of the client contacts, work description, dollar amount, periods of performance, and any other relevant information. Treasure your formal awards, and carefully copy and save any praise or accolades your company receives. All this information will help you when you must explain your past performance to future clients.

What does the government review when evaluating my past performance?

Past performance includes any relevant information about your company actions under previous government contracts. This record includes meeting contract requirements, successful performance, workmanship, customer service, cost control, scheduling, reporting, and many other factors. Every aspect of how you interact with your government client affects your ability to win future government contracts, so stay on top of your game.

Does the government have discretion or flexibility in how it evaluates past performance?

Yes, the government has considerable flexibility in how it evaluates past performance of your company. Important details about this process should be listed in the solicitation, usually in *Section L (Instructions to Offerors)* or *Section M (Evaluation Method)*.

Can the government require specific examples of past performance?

Yes, sometimes the government requests specific instances of past performance. Your company can submit a description of past performances and related information, such as the client, contract, date, location, etc. Always choose past performances where you know your company succeeded and the client was impressed.

What is a past performance questionnaire or PPQ?

Sometimes the government evaluates your past performance using questionnaires. These questionnaires are sometimes called *past performance questionnaires* or PPQs. Your company submits several past performance descriptions along with the contact information for each client. The government sends questionnaire forms to each client you chose for your past performance. The clients send the questionnaires back to the government. Your company never sees the questionnaire replies, although you can find out how the government rated or evaluated your overall past performance.

Does the government care about the recency or relevancy of the past performance?

Yes, sometimes the government discriminates between past performances by relevance or how recently the work was performed. For relevance, the government favors work in the same industry, contract type, dollar value range, etc. Work performed 10 years ago is less relevant than work performed last year. Always submit past performances that are as relevant and recent as possible.

What is CPARS?

Sometimes the government reads about your company in the *Contractor Performance Assessment Reporting System (CPARS)*. The CPARS database contains records, both positive and negative, on government contractor past performance.

If your contract is eligible, the government will enter information about your company, the contract, and your performance into CPARS. This information should be objectively based on facts, dates, data, and be verifiable. However, opinions about performance will always be somewhat subjective.

Can my company submit written comments to defend or explain itself within CPARS?

Yes, as a government contractor, you can make comments about your company in CPARS. This opportunity is available whenever the government records negative information in CPARS. Your one chance to correct the record is to state your case in writing.

Can my company ask the government to change my CPARS evaluation?

You can contact the government to try to get it to change your entire CPARS evaluation, but do not count on such a special favor. Instead, be prepared to explain your side of the story, in writing, in CPARS. The CPARS record will stand on its own, where there is information from both the government and the contractor.

How can my company prepare for CPARS evaluations?

To prepare for CPARS evaluations, your company must collect and organize important information about its performance of all its government contracts. Keep any email messages, memoranda, or documents that show praise or positive feedback from the government. If the praise comes in person or on the phone, write a memorandum to file documenting the praise.

Keep track of key dates and deliverables. Document any problems that arise and explain what your company did to help. Information like this, based on objective documents and dates, will be helpful when you need to retell your side of the story in CPARS. Keep your response objective, organized, and focused.

What is the difference between past performance and experience?

The difference between *past performance* and *experience* is simple. Experience evaluates whether your company in the past did something relevant to the upcoming government contract. Past performance evaluates how well your company performed, not just whether it did something.

If experience is a record of your attendance at school, past performance is the report card. If experience is your diploma, past performance is your actual grade point average.

What if I have no past performance?

The government can use past performance and experience as evaluation factors. If the government uses past performance, a special government rule allows your company to compete despite having no past performance.

The government wants to encourage newcomers, so a special rule states that a potential contractor with no past performance cannot be rated favorably or unfavorably on past performance. The potential contractor with no past performance must receive some sort of neutral rating on past performance.

Keep in mind that your competitors with excellent past performance retain an advantage. This special rule keeps your company from being disqualified completely. In the final decision, the government can value a positive rating on past performance more than a neutral or nonexistent rating on past performance.

What if I have no experience?

Unfortunately for you, some government contracting officers discovered a clever way to circumvent this rule. There is no saving grace for the contractor who lacks both past performance and experience. By using the evaluation factor of experience, the government can effectively discriminate against contractors with no experience.

Can I use past performance from the private sector?

You need to read the solicitation to know whether your company can use past performance from the private sector or nongovernment contracts. Sometimes you can and sometimes you cannot. The government has flexibility in how it can evaluate past performance. So, the government is free to restrict its evaluation of past performance to government contracts only. Instead, the government can open past performance evaluation to both government contracts and private sector contracts. If there is no clear distinction, submit a formal question to the contracting officer.

Is there an element of subjectivity when evaluating proposals?

Yes, subjectivity cannot be avoided when evaluating proposals, even when using defined evaluation factors. What makes a security mitigation plan good or bad? To some degree, this decision will be subjective. If the government defines what makes or breaks an evaluation factor, pay attention. If you can see no details about the evaluation factor, you must imagine yourself as the government client and think about what matters. What would be a strength or weakness? Although there may be a specific process or even formula, always remember that only human beings can make the final decision to award a government contract.

What are adjectival ratings?

Some government contracting solicitations will define the various ratings that can apply to the evaluation factors. For example, each potential contractor may receive a rating of "excellent," "good," "adequate," "marginal," or "deficient" for each evaluation factor. This rating is adjectival because it uses English-language adjectives.

What are color-based ratings?

Another way to rate potential contractors is to assign a color for each evaluation factor. Each evaluation factor will be rated as "purple," "blue," "green," "yellow," or "red." Maybe purple is the highest possible rating, and red is the lowest in the color-based rating system.

Is there any meaningful difference between using five adjectives or five colors to rate the evaluation factors?

Not really. If you think about it, there is little practical difference between these two rating systems of adjectives and colors. Both systems have five possible ratings. "Excellent" is equivalent to "purple" (the top) and "deficient" is equivalent to "red" (the bottom). This recognition leads us to an important concept.

Why should I consider ratings as merely signs or guideposts for underlying strengths and weaknesses?

Everything boils down to strengths or weaknesses — whether things are good or bad in the opinion of the government evaluator. Although ratings and evaluation factors may provide overwhelming detail, they reflect strengths or weaknesses at the simplest level.

If underlying strengths significantly outweigh weaknesses, you can expect a rating of "excellent" or "good." Conversely, where underlying weaknesses significantly outweigh strengths, you can expect a rating of "marginal" or "deficient."

Ratings are mere signs or guideposts for strengths and weaknesses to the executive who makes the final decision. The busy executive cannot be bothered to examine every detail. The government official who makes the final award decision is called the *Source Selection Authority (SSA)*. The SSA will rely on the work of other federal employees who have assigned ratings and recommended award to a specific contractor. Final ratings are valuable for the SSA because they save time and summarize the evaluation of the potential contractor. In this way, ratings are signs or guideposts for all underlying strengths and weaknesses.

What is more important, the underlying strengths and weaknesses, or the overall ratings of evaluation factors?

If there is a protest, the strengths and weaknesses matter more than ratings.

The proof for this explanation of what ratings actually mean is found in the bid protest process. When losing contractors challenge the award of a government contract, the reviewing authority will examine the underlying strengths and weaknesses, in addition to the ratings of the evaluation factors.

It is easy to understand why you must examine the underlying strengths and weaknesses. If the reviewing authority looked only at the ratings, then almost every award decision is legitimate. The winning company received all "purple" or "excellent" ratings! Isn't it easy? Of course, this outcome assumes that each rating was properly applied and based on reasonable justification. To verify this assumption, you need to examine the underlying strengths and weaknesses.

Should my proposal specifically "call out" and highlight my strengths?

Yes, strengths and weaknesses really matter. Always write your proposal and market your company with the goal of highlighting specific strengths as they relate to evaluation factors. You can even guide your government evaluators by explicitly identifying a strength and its justification: "This time-tested security mitigation plan is a significant strength because it lowers the government risk of failure and provides specific instructions for what to do during an emergency power outage." Put your company ahead of its competitors by understanding the underlying dynamics of proposal evaluations: strengths and weaknesses.

What is an oral presentation?

In some source selections, the government will require your company to provide oral presentations, which will be evaluated along with (or maybe in place of) your proposal. In plain English, an *oral presentation* means somebody from your company shows up and speaks or answers questions about your ability to perform the contract. The oral presentation may be in person, on the phone, or "virtual" by using the Internet, webcams, and microphones.

Why would the government use oral presentations?

You cannot speak to a piece of paper or a written proposal. You cannot ask probing questions, or accurately judge the knowledge of the actual human beings the proposal represents. By using oral presentations, the government can look your team members in the eye, test their technical knowledge, and ask questions that can make or break your credibility.

Who should represent my company in an oral presentation?

Choose wisely. Do not send a salesperson alone. You can send your salesperson, or business development guru, but make sure the sales team is backed up by the technical team. A common complaint of government evaluators is that the representative for the oral presentations was "all flash with no substance," and who could not answer any technical questions. Send your experts who can answer difficult questions and can speak technical jargon.

What is a debriefing?

In formal source selections under FAR Part 15, and certain task order competitions under FAR 16.505, your company may be entitled to a debriefing if you request it within a certain number of days. The *debriefing* is your opportunity to learn why you lost the contract and understand how you can prepare better proposals in the future.

What format will the government use for the debriefing?

Debriefings can be in person, over the phone, in writing, or by email communication. Contracting officers also have the discretion to perform debriefings in other formats as they see fit. Maybe the contracting officer will perform your debriefing using a webcam and microphone over the Internet.

Does the format of the debriefing matter?

Yes, the format of the debriefing will significantly affect what your company gains from the debriefing. If your debriefing is in writing, although you may be able to ask follow-up questions to the original written debriefing, nothing beats a "live" conversation. Of course, an in-person or video-streamed conversation will produce facial cues and body language that you cannot detect in writing or over the telephone. Written debriefings eliminate the possibility of "surprise questions" and revealing answers the government may withhold if they have more time for consideration, as they do in written debriefings.

Your company should request in-person debriefings whenever possible. If you cannot get an in-person debriefing, ask for a video teleconference or phone call. Your least preferred format is a debriefing in writing. The government is under no obligation to grant your request for a specific format—that is the contracting officer's decision, not yours.

What info will my company receive during the debriefing?

A *debriefing* must include at least the following info:

Significant weaknesses and deficiencies of your proposal, if any
Overall evaluated cost or price and technical rating of the winner
Overall evaluated cost or price and technical rating of your proposal
Past performance info about your company
Overall ranking of the competitors, if such a ranking occurred
Summary of the rationale for picking the winner
For commercial items, the make and model of the winner's commercial item
Reasonable responses to relevant questions about whether the source selection followed the solicitation rules, laws, regulations, and other applicable authorities

What info will you not receive during the debriefing?

The government should not provide you a point-by-point comparison of your proposal and the winning proposal. Nor should the government reveal any proprietary information, trade secrets, or the names of people who provided references for your past performance evaluation.

What is government's policy goal for conducting debriefings?

The policy goal of debriefings is to give companies info about why they lost so they can produce superior proposals in the future, with better pricing and terms. By sharing info with the losing companies, the government encourages and strengthens these companies for future contract competitions.

How do some people in industry, especially bid protest attorneys, view debriefings?

Some people in industry, especially bid protest attorneys, view debriefings as a chance to play "Gotcha!" with the government. By asking aggressive or leading questions, they try to squeeze out an admission of mistake by the government.

What is a common question some people ask in a debriefing to play the "Gotcha!" game?

The classic leading question assumes the government evaluated your company using an unstated evaluation factor, therefore opening the door to a bid protest. The aggressive debriefing attendee asks the government, "Other than the solicitation, FAR, etc., what else did the government use to rate the proposal? We just want to improve in the future."

What is the only valid governmental response to this leading question?

The only response to this leading question is something like "Nothing—the government followed the terms of the solicitation and all applicable laws and regulations."

What does the aggressive inquisitor hope the government will say in response?

The aggressive inquisitor hopes the government will fall for this trick by saying something like "Your proposal's writing style was confusing" or "I didn't like the graphics on page 25" or "Your company logo looks stupid."

What do all three of these poor responses have in common?

All three foolish responses imply the government evaluated your company using a factor that was not listed in the solicitation—a classic reason for a bid protest. Unless the solicitation listed evaluation factors like "writing style of proposal" or "beauty of graphics in proposal" or "aesthetic qualities of the company logo," the government just dug its own grave! Unstated evaluation factor is an easy bid protest win.

What is TINA?

TINA is the *Truth in Negotiations Act*. Congress passed a law which became known as the Truth in Negotiations Act to give the government a huge advantage in sole-source negotiations. Since there is no competition, the government requires the contractor to disclose the "cost or pricing data" associated with the final cost or price. This is like playing poker with your cards facing up on the table. This disclosure of cost or pricing data allows the government to look at your proprietary financial information to pressure you into a lower cost or price. If the cost or pricing data is certified, you expose your company to a significant amount of risk, so these situations should be avoided whenever possible.

Why did Congress pass TINA to level the playing field when negotiating with large defense contractors?

Large defense contractors have billions of dollars and hundreds or thousands of highly paid employees. These defense contractors run rings around the government contracting officers and program managers. There is no comparison if one side has 30 players while the other side has a team of 3.

To level the playing field, Congress passed a law which became known as the Truth in Negotiations Act or TINA. If there is competition, meaning two or more contractors, the government can assume the invisible hand of the free market pushes prices down to a competitive level. However, in a sole-source negotiation, a contractor has significant power to determine pricing. TINA diminishes that power.

Is there another name for TINA?

Yes, the Truth in Negotiations Act (TINA) was later renamed the Truthful Cost or Pricing Data Act. Most people refer to the original name, "TINA."

What does TINA require my company to disclose?

TINA requires the contractor to disclose "cost or pricing data" and to certify the data in certain circumstances. The government uses this information to negotiate with the contractor. Let's be clear about this. No company would disclose this proprietary financial information (cost or pricing data) voluntarily. This deal is bad for the contractor, but it is a significant advantage to the government.

What is cost or pricing data?

In plain English, *cost or pricing data* means all facts that a reasonable businessman would expect to affect the cost or price negotiations. Remember that key word: "facts." These facts are different from the actual price or cost. Let's also look at the Federal Acquisition Regulation (FAR) definition:

"Cost or pricing data" (10 U.S.C. 2306a(h)(1) and 41 U.S.C. chapter 35) means all facts that, as of the date of price agreement, or, if applicable, an earlier date agreed upon between the parties that is as close as practicable to the date of agreement on price, prudent buyers and sellers would reasonably expect to affect price negotiations significantly. Cost or pricing data are factual, not judgmental; and are verifiable. While they do not indicate the accuracy of the prospective contractor's judgment about estimated future costs or projections, they do include the data forming the basis for that judgment. Cost or pricing data are more than historical accounting data; they are all the facts that can be reasonably expected to contribute to the soundness of estimates of future costs and to the validity of determinations of costs already incurred."

There's a lot to unpack in that definition. Many lawsuits or claims have explored what is or is not cost or pricing data. Here are some practical examples of cost or pricing data:

Vendor quotations
Nonrecurring costs
Info on changes in production methods or purchasing volume
Data supporting projections of business prospects or objectives
Unit-cost trends such as those associated with labor efficiency
Make-or-buy decisions
Estimated resources to attain business goals
Info on management decisions that significantly affect costs

Does my cost or pricing data determine my actual price?

No! This misconception is common. The cost or pricing data consists of facts that a reasonable businessman would want to know because they would affect the negotiations. You are required to disclose these facts to the government.

You are not required to base your price on these facts (or on the cost or pricing data)! In other words, your complete cost or pricing data could lead a reasonable businessman to think that the price should be $1 million, including a tolerable profit of 20 percent. That does not mean your price must be $1 million. You can include a much higher profit and price and ask for $2 million or $20 million!

Are you saying I can price my proposal however I want, regardless of what my company submits as certified cost or pricing data?

Yes, you can price your proposal however you want. If you want to price your proposal using some other method, including methods not found in or associated with the cost or pricing data, you can do so! You can even price your proposal using strange or arbitrary methods. The government might find that strange, but you can do it! Of course, if your method or pricing is unreasonable, there is no guarantee the government will accept it.

What does "other than certified cost or pricing data" mean?

Sometimes the contractor has an exemption where it does not have to provide certified cost or pricing data. In these cases, the contracting officer may still request *other than certified cost or pricing data*. This is precisely the same information, except that your company is not required to certify the information. If this sounds like a strangely convenient benefit the government created for itself, you're on the right track.

Does my company have to submit cost or pricing data?

No, you can always refuse to submit. However, in such a case the government is likely to decline awarding you the contract.

When you are in a sole-source negotiation for a government contract, you have a lot of leverage. You are the only potential contractor. Therefore, you might be able to get away with refusing to disclose any cost or pricing data, despite what the laws and regulations require of the contracting officer.

There are also waiver procedures for the contracting officer to give your company a pass or exception to providing cost or pricing data. You are not guaranteed to get a waiver or pass. Nor are you guaranteed to get the government contract. You must analyze your competitive negotiation position and decide whether to play nice. If you push things too far, you might lose the government contract.

What is so dangerous about certified cost or pricing data?

When an employee of your company *certifies* the cost or pricing data, it creates significant risk. If the cost or pricing data is wrong or *defective*, the government can "claw back" or demand money back from your company. Your company also risks being accused of submitting a *false claim*, which is a serious charge.

For these reasons, you should always consult a competent government contracting expert when you are making decisions about certified cost or pricing data. It's also important to know the rules of whether you need to submit cost or pricing data. If you are not a rules expert, you need to hire one.

What are the exceptions for submitting certified cost or pricing data?

Laws and regulations establish several exceptions to the requirement of submitting certified cost or pricing data. If you can prove one of these exceptions, your company is legitimately excused for not providing the data.

What is the exception for adequate price competition?

If there were a competition, or the expectation of competition, then this competition is not "sole source," and your company does not have to submit certified cost or pricing data. The actual definition of "adequate price competition" is multifaceted and complex. Check each possibility of adequate price competition to see if your company can use it.

What is the exception for commercial items?

Just like with adequate price competition, the definitions (plural!) of commercial items are complex. Both products and services may qualify as commercial items.

If you are delivering a commercial product or service to the government, you do not need to disclose certified cost or pricing data. It is very common for the government and contractor to disagree about whether a product or service is properly classified as commercial. Unfortunately, the person who makes the official determination of commerciality is the government contracting officer.

What is the exception for prices set by law or regulation?

If Congress or federal agencies have defined the prices, your company does not need to provide certified cost or pricing data. For example, sometimes the prices of utilities like electricity or water are defined by law or regulation.

What is the process of obtaining a waiver?

Your company's last shot is to obtain a waiver, in writing, from the government. This requires the signature of a high-level government official. That means you may have to go "over the head" of the contracting officer. Be careful about asking for this exception to submitting certified cost or pricing data. You do not want to antagonize the contracting officer!

FAR Part 16, Types of Contracts

FAR Part 16 is a useful reference guide for the myriad types of contracts and explains how the government places orders against IDIQ contracts.

What do you mean by contract type?

Always pause and ask yourself and anyone what they mean when they refer to a "contract type." Contracts have many different attributes, including payment type, delivery type, and the type of goods or services delivered or provided under the contract. Do not mix up the different "types of types."

"Types of types!" What on Earth are you talking about?

If I asked you what type of car you drive, you could respond in several ways: "I drive a Honda." "I drive a blue car." "I drive an old car." "I drive a car with an automatic transmission."

Your car is an old, blue, Honda with an automatic transmission. We just covered four different attributes about your car (and we did not even get to the model of the car, *e.g.*, Accord!). We also just covered four different "types of types" of cars:

Brand type (Honda)
Color type (blue)
Age type (old)
Transmission type (automatic)

Government contract types pose the same problem of classification, which you can avoid by asking or answering precise questions about contract type.

How can I avoid confusion when discussing contract type?

Decide what you want to learn or share. Pause and think about whether you are exploring the payment type, delivery type, or the type of goods or services, for example.

How can I ask about payment type?

You can ask, "What is the payment type of this contract — is it fixed-price, cost-reimbursement, or time and materials?"

How can I ask about the delivery type?

You can ask, "Is this an indefinite-delivery, indefinite-quantity (IDIQ) contract or a contract with fixed delivery dates and quantities?"

How can I ask about the goods or services?

You can ask, "Is this contract for products?" or "Is this contract for services?" or "Is this a government contract for commercial items?"

I'm still confused about contract types. Can you provide more guidance?

This example will be my last to explain the different "types of types" of contract. You can find a government contract that is cost-reimbursement (payment type); that is indefinite-delivery, indefinite-quantity or IDIQ (delivery type); that delivers products (as opposed to services); and that delivers noncommercial items (as opposed to commercial items).

When someone asks a vague question about this contract — "What type of contract is it?" — what will be your answer? My answer will be: "The payment type is cost-reimbursement. The delivery type is IDIQ. The contract delivers products, and the products are noncommercial. Did you want to know about any other aspects of the contract?" Be precise!

What are the first two "families" contract payment types?

The first two "families" of contract payment types are (1) *fixed-price* and (2) *cost-reimbursement*.

What is the third "family" of contract payment types?

The third "family" of contract payment type is the *time and materials* contract, which we will discuss after fixed-price and cost-reimbursement contracts.

What are the basics of a fixed-price contract?

The bottom line is that a *fixed-price contract* provides your company a specific amount of money. No matter how much money your company actually spends to complete the contract, your company will only receive the originally specified amount. In contrast, *cost-reimbursement contracts* will pay your company based on your *actual costs incurred*. If your company spends more money than expected to complete the contract, your company might receive more money than was negotiated originally.

What are the basics of a cost-reimbursement contract?

Cost-reimbursement means the government will reimburse your costs in performing the contract, as long as they are *reasonable, allowable,* and *allocable*. For more info about reasonable, allowable, and allocable costs, read Part 30, Cost Accounting Standards Administration and Part 31, Contract Cost Principles and Procedures.

What is a cost overrun in a cost-reimbursement contract?

If your company is reimbursed for costs greater than originally negotiated, this situation is called a *cost overrun*. The actual, reimbursed costs of the contract have *overrun* the original estimated costs.

Does the government accept more risk when using a cost-reimbursement contract?

Cost-reimbursement contracts make the government nervous. The nature of the work is too complex or difficult to define properly. If the government could define exactly what work needs to be performed, your company would instead receive a fixed-price contract.

Whenever the project or work is vague and ill-defined, the government may decide to pay your company for its best efforts, rather than for a specified deliverable. Your company gets paid for all its allowable, allocable, and reasonable costs. This makes the government nervous because there is a very probable risk of a cost overrun.

What are the downsides for my company when performing cost-reimbursement contracts?

Your company faces higher levels of administrative oversight, documentation requirements, and accounting controls with cost-reimbursement contracts. The government wants to minimize the risk of a cost overrun and avoid reimbursing any inappropriate costs. To achieve these government goals, your company will be subject to a heavy administrative burden.

What types of cost accounting burdens come with cost-reimbursement contracts?

Cost-reimbursement contracts are where your company will experience the dreaded *Cost Accounting Standards* or *CAS*. In plain English, CAS is an entirely different set of accounting rules that applies only to government contracting. CAS compliance creates significant overhead costs that you will not incur for any other type of contract.

You should not use a standard accountant trained in Generally Accepted Accounting Principles. Now your company needs a specialized government contracting accountant who understands CAS. For more info, read Part 30, Cost Accounting Standards Administration and Part 31, Contract Cost Principles and Procedures.

Do I need to transform the accounting department of my company to perform cost-reimbursement contracts?

Yes, you probably need to spend money and time to get your accounting practices into compliance. For this reason, many government contractors choose to avoid cost-reimbursement contracts. The additional costs of complying with CAS, hiring a specialized government contracting accountant, and dealing with the complicated accounting requirements can be overwhelming. Before you accept your first cost-reimbursement contract, perform an economic analysis to see if the benefits outweigh the costs.

What is a cost plus fixed fee or CPFF contract?

Cost plus fixed fee or *CPFF* is the most common type of cost-reimbursement contract. In addition to the reimbursement of all reasonable, allowable, and allocable costs, your company will receive an additional fee. Your fee will be a fixed dollar amount that does not change based on your cost expenditures, unless there are new requirements added to the original contract. This means your profit margin decreases if you commit a cost overrun.

Why will cost overruns decrease my profit margin?

Here's the financial mathematics of a cost overrun. If your company spends more than the estimated cost ceiling to get the job done, this cost overrun increases the total cost of the contract, but it does not increase the fixed fee. Your original fee is a fixed dollar amount. Therefore, the ratio of the fixed fee relative to the total cost decreases, which decreases your profit margin.

For example, the total estimated cost of the contract is $1 million, and the fixed fee is $100,000. This means your fixed fee is 10 percent of the total cost. If your company commits a cost overrun, now the total cost of the contract is $1.5 million. Your company receives an extra $500,000 in reimbursed costs, which is helpful. However, now your fixed fee is less than 7 percent of the total cost. Cost overruns provide your company more revenue, but likely slimmer profit margins.

What is a cost ceiling?

In cost-reimbursement contracts, your company will be subject to an *estimated cost ceiling*. The government is not liable to pay for and you are not liable to perform work beyond this cost ceiling, unless you receive a contract modification.

What are the "Limitation of Funds" and "Limitation of Cost" clauses?

Your contract will have a *Limitation of Funds* or *Limitation of Cost* clause which forces you and the contracting officer to closely monitor the cost ceiling. Only the contracting officer has the authority to increase the cost ceiling and obligate more money on the contract. These clauses require your company to provide written notice to the government when you approach or know you will surpass the estimated cost ceiling.

What happens when my company notifies the government that our costs are close to the estimated cost ceiling?

When you notify the government that your company will exceed the cost ceiling, the government has a choice. The government can either add more money to your contract, or do nothing, which means your company will need to eventually stop work. Be sure you have written authorization to proceed from the contracting officer before you spend any money beyond the cost ceiling.

Even better, wait until you receive a signed modification to the contract. Remember, the government is not liable to pay for and you are not liable to perform work beyond the cost ceiling. Unless the cost ceiling is increased, your company will be working at risk of not being paid back or reimbursed.

Besides CPFF, are there other types of cost-reimbursement contracts?

Yes, although cost plus fixed fee or CPFF is the most common type of cost-reimbursement contract, you may encounter two other types: *incentive fee* and *award fee*.

What is an incentive fee contract?

Incentive fees are inversely proportional to the total reimbursed cost. If you commit a cost overrun, your incentive fee decreases. If you finish the contract using fewer costs than originally negotiated, your company gets a higher incentive fee.

What is an award fee contract?

Award fees are administratively decided by government committee. Every few weeks or months, the government decision makers huddle into a room and decide how much award fee to give your company. As crazy as this award fee sounds, the idea is that your company will constantly want to please the government because the next award fee meeting is just around the corner.

What does it mean to say that costs must be reasonable, allowable, and allocable?

In cost-reimbursement contracts, the government will reimburse your costs only if they are *reasonable, allowable,* and *allocable.* The contracting officer decides if the costs are *reasonable*, and the determination is mostly used as a check on ridiculous prices or unnecessary expenses.

Allocable means you can tie the costs or a portion of the costs to the particular contract you're charging them against. The cost might be 100% allocable to a single contract—a direct cost. Alternatively, the cost might be spread across several contracts—in other words, an indirect cost. The good news is the government will reimburse you for both direct and indirect costs.

Allowability is more complicated. The FAR lists allowable and unallowable costs in FAR Part 31, Contract Cost Principles and Procedures. Don't forget that your contract itself might also preclude certain costs from being reimbursed, and that contract language will trump any other guidance you find. In other words, if CAS or the FAR says the cost is allowable but your contract says the cost is unallowable, the cost is unallowable. To read more about these concepts, check out Part 30, Cost Accounting Standards Administration and Part 31, Contract Cost Principles and Procedures.

What are the benefits of fixed-price contracts?

Fixed price contracting is the land of opportunity. With greater risk comes greater reward and higher profit margins. In *firm fixed price* or *FFP* contracts, the government will only pay you a specified amount of money. If you must spend more to complete the job, it's your problem. Your profitability decreases and you can actually lose money.

On the bright side, if you can find a way to successfully perform while needing less money than the fixed price, your profit margins can be sky-high when compared to a cost-reimbursement contract. For this reason, many government contractors prefer fixed-price contracts. Furthermore, fixed-price contracts are much simpler to set up than cost-reimbursement contracts. Fixed-price contracts do not require special accountants, extra documentation, and compliance with Cost Accounting Standards.

Can the pursuit of fixed-price versus cost-reimbursement contracts change my entire organizational strategy?

Yes, the business strategies behind fixed-price and cost-reimbursement contracts are not just about economics and profit margins. Cost-reimbursement contracts require a massive amount of oversight, accounting, compliance, and record-keeping. Make sure you have the office staff or the outside consultants to help you stay compliant.

Which is simpler and requires less "back office help" — a fixed-price contract or a cost-reimbursement contract?

For most fledgling small businesses, a cost-reimbursement government contract is not a good option. Fixed-price contracts are much simpler. The transition to the first cost-reimbursement government contract should be deliberate and methodical. Plan your company growth and financial operations in a way that makes sense for the types of government contracts you expect to win.

What is a time and materials contract?

Time and materials government contracts are very similar to contracts you see for plumbers, attorneys, or car mechanics. You pay your attorney by the hour, and you pay for your attorney's costs, such as postage or court filing fees. You pay your plumber by the hour, and you pay for your plumber's costs, such as pipes, equipment, and new toilets.

When the government is the client, the government pays your company by the hour, and the government also pays for your materials used in the contract. This is the *time and materials contract.*

What is a labor-hour contract?

Labor-hour contracts are a subset of time and materials contracts. Labor-hour contracts are basically the same, except they involve no materials.

The government pays your company only by the hour, for labor. No materials exist in a labor-hour contract. For example, your labor-hour contract pays your company an hourly rate for every hour of work your employee completes onsite at the government building.

What is a fully loaded labor rate?

The *fully loaded labor rate* is the rate you bill your clients. When you win a time and materials or labor-hour government contract, you need to decide how much to bill the government per hour of work. This rate must be higher than the direct labor rate your company pays the employee. Otherwise, how can you make any money?

If you win a government contract based on time and materials, the "time" will be measured in labor hours. Your company will be paid for each hour of work and for any materials used. Each hour of work will be classified according to a labor category and labor rate. Your experienced employees will have a more expensive labor rate because they cost you more to employ. Your cheaper employees will have a cheaper labor rate.

Can you provide an example of calculating the fully loaded labor rate?

If your company pays one employee $50 per hour, you need to bill that employee's labor hours at a higher labor rate, otherwise your company will not make a profit. Start with the $50 per hour (direct cost), then apply the indirect costs of that employee and add profit for your company. Let's say your indirect costs per labor hour is $10. Your profit per labor hour is $5. Now you have a fully loaded labor rate:

Direct labor rate (what you pay the employee) + indirect costs + profit = fully loaded labor rate

$50 + $10 + $5 = $65

Mathematically restated, this equation transforms into:

Fully loaded labor rate − indirect costs − profit = direct labor rate your company pays the employee

$65 − $10 − $5 = $50

See how it all adds up?

The fully loaded labor rate captures the individual, direct, hourly labor rate for a particular labor category, along with the indirect costs and profit for your company. In time and materials contracts, you must always bill your labor rates as fully loaded labor rates. Otherwise, you will shortchange your company.

Following the earlier example, if you billed your employee at $50 per hour on a time and materials contract, this would be a rookie mistake. You forgot to add the indirect costs and your company profit.

Why is it so important to bill the fully loaded labor rate in time and materials or labor-hour contracts?

If you fail to bill for the fully loaded rate, you will fail to earn a sustainable profit. You must propose, quote, bill, and charge fully loaded labor rates in your time and materials contracts. Make sure the fully loaded labor rate captures all costs for that employee's labor category: direct costs, indirect costs, fringe benefits like healthcare, etc. Of course, don't forget profit! Your company needs a government contracting expert or accountant to help you with these cost calculations.

What is a wrap rate?

The *wrap rate* is the multiplier your company uses to transform the employee's direct, hourly cost into a fully loaded labor rate. In the earlier example, the wrap rate is calculated by dividing the fully loaded labor rate by the direct cost of $50 per hour.

Wrap rate = fully loaded labor rate / direct labor rate

1.3 = $65 / $50

$65 is 130% of $50

In this example, the wrap rate or wrap multiplier is 1.3 or 130%. The fully loaded labor rate is 130% of the direct labor rate your company pays the employee. If you multiply the direct labor rate by 1.3, you arrive at the fully loaded labor rate.

What if my wrap rates are too high?

If your company has a high wrap rate, it means you have relatively greater indirect costs and profit that you apply to create fully loaded labor rates. This can be a disadvantage because your competitors can submit lower bids by using lower wrap rates. You can be "underbid" and lose the government contract.

What if my wrap rates are too low?

If your company has a low wrap rate, it means you have relatively less indirect costs and profit. Maybe you can "underbid" your competitors, but maybe your profit margins are smaller.

What is the ideal wrap rate?

There is no such thing as an ideal wrap rate that applies to any company in any industry performing on any contract. The ideal wrap rate is affected by too many factors including the work performed, your competitors, market conditions, and your company's financial position. The only honest answer is "it depends on many factors."

Fine-tuning your wrap rates is an extremely important part of winning government contracts. You need to find a balance between profitability and competitive pricing — the "sweet spot" of wrap rates.

What is an indefinite-delivery, indefinite-quantity or IDIQ contract?

An *indefinite-delivery, indefinite-quantity* or *IDIQ contract* allows agencies the flexibility to place orders for the amounts they need when the need arises. If the agency knew it needed 1,000 computers in 30 days, the agency could sign a simple purchase order for 1,000 computers. This purchase order would have a definite quantity (1,000) and a definite delivery schedule (within the next 30 days).

But what if the agency knows it needs between 1,000 and 1,000,000 computers at various points within the next 5 years? Enter the IDIQ contract, which establishes a minimum and maximum quantity (between 1,000 and 1,000,000) and an ordering period (today through the next 5 years). Through this IDIQ contract, the agency can easily satisfy its needs for computers whenever they arise. Next month, the agency can order 2,000 computers. The following month, the agency can place zero orders. At the end of next year, the agency can order 30,000 computers. This flexibility is very convenient for the agency and the contracting office.

If you remember our earlier discussion about the "types of types" of contracts, the IDIQ description pertains to the delivery type.

Can an IDIQ contract have different payment types?

Great question! You understood the earlier lesson about "types of types." Yes, IDIQ contracts can have fixed-price or cost-reimbursement payment types. So, there are fixed-price, IDIQ contracts and there are cost-reimbursement, IDIQ contracts.

What is a single-award, IDIQ contract?

A single-award, IDIQ contract is held by one company, rather than multiple companies. For example, company ABC wins the only IDIQ contract to deliver computer laptops. Company ABC will "win" every order placed against the single-award IDIQ contract.

What is a multiple-award, IDIQ contract?

Multiple-award, IDIQ contracts are awarded to two or more companies, rather than a single company. For example, the government wants to diversify its suppliers of computer laptops. So, the government awards three multiple-award, IDIQ contracts to company DEF, company XYZ, and company QRS.

How does the government decide which of the three companies wins each order?

Usually, the government will compete each order among the three companies. The terms of the multiple-award, IDIQ contract will usually require the government to give each of the three companies a *fair opportunity*.

What is "fair opportunity?"

Fair opportunity is a special standard of competition that applies to multiple-award contracts, like multiple-award, IDIQ contracts. This competition standard of fair opportunity is different from the "full and open competition" required by FAR Part 15 and the "maximum extent practicable" required for simplified acquisition procedures under FAR Part 13.

The competition standard of fair opportunity applies exclusively to multiple-award contracts. Under fair opportunity, the government must notify each contract-holder, but not any other companies. Therefore, if your company failed to win one of the original multiple-award contracts, you are ineligible to win any orders placed against the multiple-award contracts. Only the contract-holders have a "fair opportunity" to win the orders.

What is an indefinite-delivery, definite-quantity contract?

An *indefinite-delivery, definite-quantity contract* is very similar to an IDIQ contract. The important difference is the government knows the exact quantity of supplies or services but does not know when they need to be delivered or performed. This difference is spelled out in the names:

Indefinite-delivery, indefinite quantity (IDIQ): "I don't know how much I need or when I need it." Indefinite-delivery, definite quantity: "I know how much I need, but I don't know when I need it."

What is a requirements contract?

A *requirements contract* is awarded to a single company to provide all the government's needs for a supply or service during a specific period. You should celebrate if your company wins a requirements contract.

FAR PART 17, SPECIAL CONTRACTING METHODS

FAR Part 17 explains how options work in government contracting.

What is an option period in the context of government contracting?

Most government contracts are for a total of 5 years. The 5 years are usually separated into 1-year periods of performance. The first year is the *base period* and starts shortly after you sign the contract. The next 4 years are *option periods*. When you signed the contract, your company also agreed to the possibility of performing the option periods.

What is a Contract Line Item Number or CLIN?

Most government contracts use *Contract Line Item Numbers (CLINs)* to track different goods or services provided under the contract. Under the usual numbering convention, the base period of performance will be numbered CLIN 0001. The first option period will be CLIN 1001, the second will be CLIN 2001, the third will be CLIN 3001, and the fourth will be CLIN 4001. So, the typical numbering convention starts with "0" for the base period, "1" for the first option, "2" for the second option, and so on. Sometimes the numbers will be different, but this is the most common arrangement.

The second, third, fourth, and fifth periods of performance are option periods, meaning the government has the unilateral choice ("option") to continue performance or not. Your company started performance under the base period, CLIN 0001, shortly after signing the contract. However, your company may perform some, all, or none of the option periods, depending on the decisions of the government.

The government gets your company to continue performance through the option periods by *exercising* an option. If the government does not exercise the next option period, your contractual obligations to perform are finished.

What does it mean to exercise an option?

Exercise an option is a fancy term for when the government orders your company to perform an option. Some people describe it as "activating" the option period or "turning on" the option CLIN. Your company will receive a written modification to the contract which exercises the option period.

Is the government required to exercise any option under my contract?

No, because if the government were somehow required to exercise an option, then it would be an obligation, not an option. The government has the *unilateral right* to exercise any option.

What do you mean by unilateral right?

The government's right to exercise the option is *unilateral* because your company cannot reject the exercised option. Your company need not sign or agree to anything. The government sends you a written modification that exercises the option, and your company is obligated to perform.

Are you saying my company cannot refuse an exercised option, even if I do not want the work?

Yes, your company must perform any option the government (properly) exercises.

What happens if my company refuses to perform the exercised option?

If your company refuses to perform a properly exercised option, your company failed to follow the terms of the contract you signed. When you fail to perform, you risk being *terminated for default*. Read more about this concept in Part 49, Termination of Contracts.

Will my company get advance notification before the government exercises the option?

Yes, the standard FAR clause for options requires the government to notify your company in writing of its intent to exercise the option.

How far in advance will my company be notified in writing?

Read the options clause in your contract. The advance notification timeline can be tailored or changed by the contracting officer, so you need to check your contract. Some contracting officers write in a notification timeline of 30 days before exercising the option. Others will notify your company 15 days in advance. I have seen many government contracts that require advance notice of only 1 day before, and even a few that allow *any time* before the option period of performance. For these reasons, you need to mark your calendar after you check your government contracts so that you will never be surprised by an option period. You should also mark your calendar so that if you fail to receive a notification of the intent to exercise the option, you can contact the government to determine if it happened by mistake or by design.

Are you saying the government sometimes forgets to exercise an option?

Yes, I am warning you the government sometimes forgets to exercise an option. Your company should stay on top of the dates and immediately contact the contracting officer if you think you're missing a notification or option exercise. You may save yourself from losing a valuable contract and save the contracting officer from embarrassment and inconvenience.

What happens if the contracting officer forgets to exercise the option in time?

Options must be exercised in precisely the same way they were negotiated in the contract. If the contracting officer fails to follow any material condition, such as the notification requirement, the government loses the *unilateral right* to exercise the option. In other words, your company is no longer obligated to perform the option period.

Can my company "walk away" from the contract if the government fails to exercise the option properly?

Yes, if the government forgets or fails to exercise your option in time, your company has a choice. You can walk away, with no penalties. The government cannot force you to perform because it lost the *unilateral right* to exercise the option.

Instead, you can negotiate with the government to sign a *bilateral modification* (signed by your company and the government) that "re-creates" the option period to fix the mistake. Some contracting officers or government attorneys will say you cannot fix the mistake and you must solicit, compete, and sign an entirely new contract. Your company cannot do much about risk-averse government employees, but you could persistently request a modification to your current contract.

Is it a bad sign if the government does not exercise my option and that choice was not a mistake?

Yes, if the government purposefully declined to exercise your option, that choice is a very bad sign for your company. For some reason, the government does not want your company to perform the remaining periods of the contract. Maybe you failed to satisfy the government. Maybe the government officials think they can get a better deal elsewhere. Maybe the government no longer needs the subject of the contract. In any case, your company loses future revenue.

What must the government consider before exercising any option?

Before exercising any option, the contracting officer must consider a long list of items and must formalize the decision in writing. This determination memo must affirm that:

Money is available
Government still needs the subject of the contract
Exercising the option is preferable to looking for alternate sources
Government evaluated the contractor's past performance
Contractor performed the contract adequately so far
Contractor has no disqualifying info in the System for Award Management

FAR Part 18, Emergency Acquisitions

FAR Part 18 identifies special flexibilities for emergency acquisitions, such as contracting within disaster areas or warzones.

What situations qualify as an emergency acquisition?

Several situations qualify as emergencies that allow for special contracting flexibilities. These situations include:

Presidential declaration of an emergency or major disaster
Contingency operations
Secretary of State requests international disaster assistance for another nation
Contracts to defend or recover from cyber, nuclear, biological, chemical, or radiological attacks against the United States

What is a contingency operation?

Contingency operation is a fancy term for operations within or near dangerous warzones.

Can you provide an example of a situation that qualified as an emergency and allowed for special contracting flexibilities?

In 2005, the destruction caused by Hurricane Katrina led President George W. Bush to declare a state of emergency in Louisiana, which activated the special contracting flexibilities found in FAR Part 18, Emergency Acquisitions.

What contracting flexibilities are available for emergency acquisitions?

Many! Most of these contracting flexibilities allow for a significant increase in the dollar value threshold for using certain contracting procedures. For example, emergencies allow for a larger dollar threshold for using simplified acquisition procedures.

The intent behind these policies is to acquire goods and services faster in an emergency. Other flexibilities include the ability to waive or relax documentation or procedural requirements. Again, the policy is to speed things along to respond quickly to the emergency. Understandably, the priority is to save lives, not "check the boxes" on the forms or write memos.

What flexibility is available for responses to disaster areas or local emergencies?

Read more about the *Robert T. Stafford Disaster Relief and Emergency Assistance Act* in Part 26, Other Socioeconomic Programs.

Are there contracting flexibilities available at the discretion of the contracting officer or federal agency?

Yes, not all the contracting flexibilities in FAR Part 18 require a Presidential declaration of emergency or the like. FAR Part 18 provides a long list of flexibilities available at the discretion of the agency or contracting officer. These flexibilities include:

Limiting sources or limiting competition for urgent situations
Using "letter contracts" and negotiating definite details later
Waiving various qualification or procedural requirements
Overriding the automatic "freeze" during a protest
Extraordinary contract powers discussed in FAR Part 50
Awarding to contractors not registered in the System for Award Management

FAR Part 19, Small Business Programs

FAR Part 19 explains how the government encourages the award of prime contracts and subcontracts to small businesses and other socioeconomic categories.

What is the "big picture" for small business contracting and small business set-asides?

A *small business set-aside* means the government reserved a contract exclusively for small businesses. Only small businesses can submit a proposal and win the contract.

Is there a specific goal for how many contracts should be set aside for small businesses?

Yes, small businesses are supposed to receive about 23 percent of all eligible government contracts each year. Yet small businesses are not the only category eligible for contract set-asides. Other categories, which are subsets of the general category of small business, also have set-aside goals.

Can the government meet its set-aside goals by "counting twice" for a company that qualifies as both a small business and some other category?

Yes, for example, a women-owned small business also qualifies as a small business. The women-owned small business can compete for contracts that are set aside either for small businesses or women-owned small businesses. If the women-owned small business wins a contract that was set-aside for women-owned small businesses, the government counts that contract award towards both goals: small businesses and women-owned small businesses.

What are the other socioeconomic categories that receive special preferences in government contracting?

The variety of small business and socioeconomic categories can be overwhelming:

-small business (SB)
-veteran-owned small business (VOSB)
-service-disabled, veteran-owned small business (SDVOSB)
-women-owned small business (WOSB)
-economically disadvantaged, women-owned small business (EDWOSB)
-historically underutilized business zone small business (HUBZone)
-Small Business Administration's 8(a) business development program (8a)
-small disadvantaged business (SDB)

How can my company qualify as a small business?

Small business has a very specific meaning in government contracting. Just because you consider your business to be a small business does not mean you are eligible for small business set-asides. Instead, small businesses are defined by their number of employees or revenue. Each small business set-aside contract will list a *North American Industry Classification System (NAICS)* code.

What is a NAICS code?

NAICS codes consist of six numbers. The government uses NAICS codes to classify companies and to track economic data. In government contracting, the NAICS code really matters in determining what standards a small business must meet to qualify for a small business set-aside contract. These NAICS code standards rely on employee count and average revenue.

The NAICS code determines the revenue or employee limitations that apply to that particular set-aside. For example, one NAICS code has an employee limit of 50. Another NAICS code has a revenue limit of $500 million.

How can I calculate my company's revenue and number of employees?

The rules are subject to change by the Small Business Administration. The latest rule is to calculate the average of the last 5 years of revenue. The previous rule was to calculate the average of the last 3 years of revenue.

You count your employees by finding the average number of employees per pay period of the last year. Prorate the number of pay periods and employees if your company is less than 1 year old. Distinguish employees from *independent contractors* (nonemployees like subcontractors or vendors) using the same factors that the Internal Revenue Service uses for taxation purposes.

How does the NAICS code relate to a small business set-aside?

Each NAICS code corresponds to a particular industry subset. For example, there is a NAICS code for computer hardware and a NAICS code for custom computer programming services. There is also a NAICS code for management consulting. Your company can qualify as a small business under several different NAICS codes. Or your company may qualify under no NAICS codes if it exceeds all the relevant size and revenue standards. In contrast, the smallest companies may qualify under every single NAICS code.

Your company is only a *small business* for government contract set-asides that designate the particular NAICS codes that qualify you as a small business. In other words, you must read each government contract set-aside, look for the NAICS code, and confirm that your company qualifies as a small business under that particular NAICS code.

If the set-aside contract specifies a NAICS code that qualifies you as a small business, you are eligible as a prime contractor. If the set-aside contract designates one of the NAICS codes that does not qualify you as a small business, you are not eligible.

Again, your company is a *small business* only under certain NAICS codes. The only way for your company to be a "universal small business" under every NAICS code—with no possibility of being considered a large business—is if your company employee count and revenue are below every single NAICS code standard that exists.

Is there a recognized category of companies that do not qualify as small businesses, but are not "large" businesses?

No, there is no "medium-sized business" category in government contracting. You are either a small business or a large business. If you do not qualify under a specific set-aside and the associated NAICS code, you are a large business for that opportunity. It does not matter whether you qualify as a small business for any other opportunities.

Should my company stay small, or grow large?

Many companies choose to "stay small" by turning down government contracting opportunities or by hiring no extra employees. Receiving set-aside contracts is such a tremendous advantage that many companies plan to remain small indefinitely. Other companies plan to be acquired or bought out by larger competitors once they reach a certain milestone.

What are the risks of growing from a small business to a large business?

The transition from a small business to a large business can be risky. Once you are no longer a small business, you compete with very large companies such as Boeing and Lockheed Martin. Without the soft, warm embrace of small business set-asides, you face the cold reality of competition at the highest level of government contracting. This change can be abrupt within your business lifecycle. Plan ahead.

Who assigns my company its NAICS codes?

Nobody assigns a NAICS code or NAICS codes to your company. You self-assign your company one or more NAICS codes. Your primary NAICS code should be whatever activity dominates or generates the most revenue for your business. Although you can assert whatever NAICS codes you want, remember that competitors can challenge your status as a small business under a particular NAICS code.

What are the small business and socioeconomic categories and whom do they benefit?

VOSB: Veteran-owned small businesses are owned and controlled by veterans of the United States military. The policy purpose is to help veterans in government contracting.

SDVOSB: Service-disabled, veteran-owned small businesses are owned and controlled by veterans who have a documented disability resulting from their service in the US military. The policy purpose is to help service-disabled veterans in government contracting.

WOSB: Women-owned small businesses are owned and controlled by women, of course. The policy purpose is to help women in government contracting.

EDWOSB: Economically disadvantaged, women-owned small businesses are owned and controlled by women who qualify under certain wealth or income limitations. The policy purpose is to help relatively poor women in government contracting.

HUBZone: Historically underutilized business zone small businesses must be located in poor, underdeveloped, or damaged areas. The policy purpose is to increase employment opportunities, investment, and economic development in specific areas. You can research what areas qualify as HUBZones on the Small Business Administration website. You might be surprised at what areas qualify. For example, about one-half of Washington, DC qualifies as a HUBZone.

8(a) business development program: The name comes from Section 8(a) of the Small Business Act. The 8(a) program helps small disadvantaged businesses grow and compete in government contracting. The 8(a) company is eligible for procurement assistance, business consulting, financial assistance, and other advantages provided by the Small Business Administration. The hope is that after years of this help from the Small Business Administration, the 8(a) company will be able to compete in the open market.

SDB: Small disadvantaged businesses are owned and controlled by socially and economically disadvantaged people. These standards are subject to change, such as the specific net worth and total assets limitations to qualify as economically disadvantaged. Socially disadvantaged individuals currently means people who have been subjected to racial or ethnic prejudice or cultural bias within American society because of their identities as members of groups and without regard to their individual qualities. The social disadvantage must stem from circumstances beyond their control. Currently, the Small Business Administration presumes that these groups are socially disadvantaged: African American, Native American, Asian-Pacific American, Subcontinent Asian American, and other groups specially designated by the Small Business Administration. People not clearly in these presumptive groups must prove their disadvantage by submitting evidence.

What are the Limitations on Subcontracting clauses?

When the government awards your company a contract, it wants your company to perform most of the contract. Your company cannot subcontract away too much of the work, depending on the situation. This simple principle is enforced by the *Limitations on Subcontracting clauses*. There are several versions of this clause, and the clause operates differently depending on the specific type of contract, but this chapter provides the basics.

What is the policy goal behind the Limitations on Subcontracting clauses?

Small business set-asides are supposed to benefit small businesses. Women-owned small business set-asides are supposed to benefit women-owned small businesses. This policy is easy to understand.

If the government awards a small business set-aside but the small business subcontracts 90 percent of the work to a large company like Boeing, something is probably wrong. Boeing gets the benefit of the set-aside instead of the small business. For this reason, there are specific limitations on how much your company can subcontract if it receives a set-aside.

Is there more than one version of the Limitations on Subcontracting clause?

Yes, there are several versions of the Limitations on Subcontracting clause. You must know which version of the clause is in your contract. Pay attention to the date at the end of the title of the clause. Over time, these clauses change. Although the title may be the same, the substance of a clause can become different.

How much of the prime contract must my company perform when subject to one of the Limitations on Subcontracting clauses?

Again, each version of the Limitations on Subcontracting clause is slightly different. There are differing percentage limitations and differing ways to calculate the percentage. Some calculate based on money paid to employees, some allow contractors to subtract the cost of materials, and some examine total contract values rather than company expenses. Generally, these Limitations on Subcontracting clauses prohibit your company from subcontracting away more than 50 percent or one-half of the contract.

Sometimes the percentage limitation is greater than 50 percent. In those cases, your company can subcontract away more work. For example, construction contracts have more flexibility because it's common for complex construction projects to have many different subcontractors.

Should my company's teaming agreements consider the Limitations on Subcontracting clauses?

Yes, when your company negotiates and signs teaming agreements to work together with other government contractors, beware the Limitations on Subcontracting clauses. Beware companies that offer subcontractors to perform more than 50 percent of the work for set-aside prime contracts. Such companies may promise more than they can deliver.

Your teaming agreement exists between your company and the other contractor, but the government may cause problems. If the government enforces the Limitations on Subcontracting against the prime contractor, the prime contractor may choose to violate the teaming agreement to satisfy the government. Avoid messy situations by anticipating which version of the Limitations on Subcontracting clause will apply to the prime contractor.

Does the Limitations on Subcontracting clause apply to all government contracts?

No, the Limitations on Subcontracting clause does not apply to government contracts that are not set aside for small businesses. However, some similar limitations often apply to any other government contract.

What is the Limitations on Pass-Through Charges clause?

The *Limitations on Pass-Through Charges clause* is similar to the Limitations on Subcontracting clause. The difference is that the Limitations on Pass-Through Charges clause can be inserted into government contracts that are not set aside for small businesses.

The similarity between the two clauses is that they both create strict limitations on how much work the prime contractor can subcontract. A second similarity is that both clauses enforce the government expectation that any company that receives a contract will perform a significant amount of the work.

What is the policy goal for the Limitations on Pass-Through Charges clause?

The Limitations on Pass-Through Charges clause prevents a prime contractor from getting the government to pay for the middleman. In this discussion, the "middleman" does not provide value and collects fees only by connecting the government to a lower-tier subcontractor.

The government expects subcontracting, but it does not want to pay excessive fees to middleman government contractors. This is the purpose of the Limitations on Pass-Through Charges clause.

Always read the specific language of this clause, but it generally requires the prime contractor to report to the contracting officer if any subcontractor will perform more than 70 percent of the work. It also requires a report if any lower tier subcontractor will perform more than 70 percent of the work of the higher tier subcontractor.

The Limitations on Pass-Through Charges clause prohibits the government from paying "excessive" pass-through charges. The trigger for investigating whether pass-through charges are "excessive" is any subcontract for more than 70 percent of the work.

You must distinguish between the threshold for notification (70 percent) and the prohibition on paying "excessive" pass-through charges. "Excessive" is a relative and subjective term. The government contracting officer will determine whether the pass-through charges are excessive. Sometimes the government will pay pass-through charges if the contracting officer determines they are not excessive.

FAR Part 20, Reserved

FAR Part 20 is reserved. Nothing to see here! FAR Part 20 has no text because it is reserved for future use.

Check out my online courses available at **Courses.ChristophLLC.com**.

Have you read my first book, the bestselling Government Contracts in Plain English? Get your copy at **https://www.amazon.com/dp/173419815X/**

You should also read my third book, Government Contracts Negotiation, Simplified! Buy your copy at **https://www.amazon.com/dp/1734198133**

Buy all the books in *The Government Contracts in Plain English Series*, available at **https://www.amazon.com/dp/B09MRCMWBD?binding=paperback**

When you need my help, email me at **Christoph@ChristophLLC.com**

FAR Part 21, Reserved

FAR Part 21 is reserved. Nothing to see here! FAR Part 21 has no text because it is reserved for future use.

Check out my online courses available at **Courses.ChristophLLC.com**.

Have you read my first book, the bestselling Government Contracts in Plain English? Get your copy at **https://www.amazon.com/dp/173419815X/**

You should also read my third book, Government Contracts Negotiation, Simplified! Buy your copy at **https://www.amazon.com/dp/1734198133**

Buy all the books in *The Government Contracts in Plain English Series*, available at **https://www.amazon.com/dp/B09MRCMWBD?binding=paperback**

When you need my help, email me at **Christoph@ChristophLLC.com**

FAR Part 22, Application of Labor Laws to Government Acquisitions

FAR Part 22 prescribes policy for the implementation of labor laws in government contracts.

What is the Service Contract Act?

Note: The *Service Contract Act* was renamed to the *Service Contract Labor Standards*. We will use the original name of the *Service Contract Act (SCA)*. The SCA is a law passed by Congress that applies to certain government contracts that use "service employees."

Under the SCA, what is a service employee?

The SCA has a misleading title, which sounds like it applies to any contractor employee performing services. However, "service employee" has several exemptions, including certain executive, administrative, or professional employees. For example, most white-collar, knowledge-based services (KBS) are exempt under these exemptions.

What are some examples of service employees that are covered by the SCA?

Some examples of services covered by the SCA include:

Cafeteria and food services
Janitorial and custodial services
Trash removal
Landscaping
Warehousing or storage
Guard and watchman security service
Laundry and dry cleaning
Packing and crating
Parking services

Does the SCA apply to contracts that are not government contracts?

No, the SCA applies only to certain contracts issued by the United States federal government and the District of Columbia.

How does the SCA protect these service employees?

The SCA requires your company to pay these employees the *prevailing wages* and benefits in the local region. The Department of Labor issues a *wage determination* that defines the minimum level of wage you must pay these workers to satisfy the "prevailing wages." In some contracts above a certain dollar threshold, the SCA also requires your company to pay overtime of 150% of the worker's regular pay rate for any hours worked beyond 40 hours in a workweek. In this way, the SCA prevents contractors from undercutting the wages and benefits of its service employees.

What is the Davis-Bacon Act?

Think of the *Davis-Bacon Act (DBA)* as a variation of the SCA used for government contracts for construction. While the SCA protects service employees, the DBA protects construction workers on certain government contracts.

How does the DBA protect construction workers on certain government contracts?

Like the SCA, the DBA requires your company to pay covered employees the prevailing wages and benefits in the local region. Once again, the Department of Labor determines the prevailing wages and benefits for the local region. In some contracts above a certain dollar threshold, the DBA also requires your company to pay overtime of 150% of the worker's regular pay rate for any hours worked beyond 40 hours in a workweek.

What is the Walsh-Healey Public Contracts Act?

Think of the *Walsh-Healey Public Contracts Act (PCA)* as a variation of the SCA used for government contracts for manufacturing, or for furnishing materials, supplies, articles, or equipment.

How does the PCA protect these manufacturing, materials, supplies, articles, or equipment employees?

Unlike the SCA and DBA, the PCA does not use a prevailing wages analysis. Instead, the PCA requires your company to pay covered employees the federal minimum wage from the Fair Labor Standards Act (FLSA) and overtime pay of 150% of the regular pay rate for any hours worked beyond 40 hours in a workweek. The PCA also sets certain safety and health standards for your covered employees.

What do the Service Contract Act, Davis-Bacon, and Walsh-Healey laws have in common?

Each of these laws, applicable to certain government contracts, protect American workers by setting standards for wages, benefits, safety precautions, or work schedules. SCA protects contractors qualifying as service employees. DBA protects contractor employees in construction and related activities. PCA protects contractor employees in manufacturing, materials, supplies, articles, or equipment activities.

When my company hires subcontractors, what happens if the subcontractors violate the SCA, DBA, or PCA?

As the prime contractor, you are responsible for compliance or noncompliance of your subcontractor. Now you know one more reason to screen and monitor your subcontractors thoroughly when they perform federal contracts.

Why should government contractors be concerned about compliance with the SCA, DBA, and PCA?

Violating any of these worker-protection laws can result in steep fines, protracted audits, payment of back wages or benefits, or other problems for your company. Ignorance is no excuse. Your employees can report suspected violations to the Department of Labor, which can also perform random audits of your company at any time.

If your government contract involves certain types of services, construction, or manufacturing, you need to hire expert professional help to keep your company compliant. Do not try to "figure it out yourself" — that would be a grave mistake.

FAR Part 23, Environment, Energy and Water Efficiency, Renewable Energy Technologies, Occupational Safety, and Drug-Free Workplace

FAR Part 23 explains environmental, drug, and safety policies for government contractors.

What does "progress" mean to Congress regarding contracting policy?

Congress demonstrates a familiar pattern in federal contracting policy. Congress passes a law to advance some political agenda. Federal agencies implement this law by creating or revising a regulation in the FAR, often a standard contract clause. Federal contractors comply with the standard contract clause from the FAR if it is found within their contracts. At the end of this exercise, Congress declares victory because there is a new FAR clause that contracting officers are supposed to insert into federal contracts. "Progress!"

Is the FAR clause that requires contractors to ban texting while driving an example of this "progress?"

Definitely. Congress "solved" the dangerous problem of texting on a cell phone while driving. Everyone agrees that distractions during driving are dangerous. Texting is a common distraction. So, Congress passed several laws against texting and driving. One of these laws is implemented into a standard contract clause in the FAR that requires federal contractors to ban their employees from texting while driving on duty. "Progress!"

What is the government's policy on federal contractors having a drug-free workplace?

Most government contracts require inclusion of the Drug-Free Workplace clause. You should modify your company's *Contractor Code of Business Ethics and Conduct* to comply, verbatim, with the Drug-Free Workplace clause. Read more about this code in FAR Part 3, Improper Business Practices and Personal Conflicts of Interest.

Should I modify my Contractor Code of Business Ethics and Conduct to comply with the ban on texting while driving?

Yes, you should. While we are on the topic, you should modify or supplement your Contractor Code of Business Ethics and Conduct to comply with all such FAR clauses. Consider your code to be the "one stop shop" to comply with several different FAR clauses.

If the FAR clauses require or forbid certain behavior from your employees, find a way to write it into your Contractor Code of Business Ethics and Conduct. Make your employees read and sign the Code. Hire a professional to provide training, compliance, and oversight for your company's Code.

What are the environmental requirements for government contractors?

Too many to name or summarize in this "highlight reel." Read through your contracts and make sure you understand them enough to comply.

If you have questions about compliance with any of your contract terms or clauses, email me at **Christoph@ChristophLLC.com**.

FAR Part 24, Protection of Privacy and Freedom of Information

FAR Part 24 provides details about Freedom of Information Act (FOIA) requests.

What is the Freedom of Information Act?

The *Freedom of Information Act* or *FOIA* is a law passed by Congress in the aftermath of the Watergate scandal in the time of President Richard Nixon. Among other things, FOIA requires the federal government to disclose certain documents or general information if the public requests it formally.

All kinds of interesting revelations about the federal government have sprung forth from American citizens exercising their rights under FOIA. American citizens write to federal agencies, requesting certain documents or information, justifying their request using FOIA, and federal agencies deliver dutifully. There have been FOIA requests on unidentified flying objects (UFO), plane crashes, interrogation techniques, and many other provocative topics.

How are FOIA requests relevant to government contractors?

You can use FOIA requests to gather business intelligence on your clients and competitors. If there is no easier way to obtain information about your competitors, FOIA can force the government to divulge information about the current or prior contractor as well as the federal contract itself, within certain limitations.

FAR Part 25, Foreign Acquisition

FAR Part 25 prescribes policy for acquiring foreign supplies, services, and construction materials, as well as policy for contracts performed outside the United States.

Are the rules different for government contracts performed outside the United States?

Yes.

Are there special rules for government contracts for foreign supplies, services, and construction materials that are used by the United States?

Yes.

Are there special rules for government contracts performed in war zones?

Yes, and some other names for these contracts are *contingency operations* or *contingency contracts*.

What are some of the laws and regulations discussed or implemented in FAR Part 25?

Buy American Act (BAA)
Trade Agreements Act (TAA)
International Traffic in Arms Regulation (ITAR)

Should I hire several other professionals to advise me?

Yes.

Why are your answers about these topics so short?

All of these are serious issues that require the assistance of a professional rather than skimming through a book of FAQs. If you're exporting, importing, selling weapons, or contracting overseas or in war zones, you need to hire help. Don't be cheap. Pay for the best help you can afford so you can stay out of trouble.

FAR PART 26, OTHER SOCIOECONOMIC PROGRAMS

FAR Part 26 explains the Indian Incentive Program and the Stafford Act.

Why are these socioeconomic programs not in FAR Part 19, Small Business Programs?

Great question! I have no idea. It seems like the socioeconomic programs in FAR Part 26 are like the socioeconomic programs found in FAR Part 19, Small Business Programs. For some reason unknown to me, the programs in FAR Part 26 have their own section. Perhaps they should be consolidated into FAR Part 19.

What is the Indian Incentive Program?

The *Indian Incentive Program* encourages prime contractors to issue subcontracts to Indian organizations and Indian-owned economic enterprises. The policy goal is to help the American Indian communities by stimulating economic activity (in the form of government contracting).

How does the Indian Incentive Program work?

If your prime contract includes the clause for the Indian Incentive Program, your company receives a payment equal to five percent of the amount paid to a subcontractor that qualifies as an Indian organization or Indian-owned economic enterprise. In this way, the prime contractor gets "bonus money" for awarding subcontracts to Indian organizations or Indian-owned economic enterprises. The "bonus money" is equal to five percent of the amount paid to the eligible subcontractor.

Who pays the prime contractor for subcontracting to Indian organizations or Indian-owned economic enterprises?

The federal government pays the five percent "bonus money" to the prime contractor after receiving, evaluating, and approving the request from the prime contractor.

What is the Robert T. Stafford Disaster Relief and Emergency Assistance Act?

The *Robert T. Stafford Disaster Relief and Emergency Assistance Act* is also called the *Stafford Act*. Such natural disasters as earthquakes, hurricanes, and tornados destroy property, people, and also economic prospects for the affected locality. The Stafford Act encourages government contracting in these major disaster or emergency areas so that the local community can rebuild and revive its local economy.

How does the Stafford Act encourage government contracting in major disaster or emergency areas?

The Stafford Act allows the contracting officer to establish a preference for local companies, individuals, and organizations to win federal contracts for disaster or emergency response activities. For example, contracts for debris clearance, distribution of supplies, or reconstruction all qualify as emergency response activities.

What kind of preference does the Stafford Act provide for local companies?

There are two types of preference under the Stafford Act: evaluation preference and set-asides. An evaluation preference means that local companies get a higher evaluation rating because they are local, providing them a distinct advantage in competitive contracts. A local area set-aside is much stronger and means that *only* local companies are eligible for the contracts, reserving the contracts *exclusively* for local companies. When using an evaluation preference, nonlocal companies can win the contracts. When using a local area set-aside, nonlocal companies are barred from the competition.

What qualifies as a major disaster or emergency?

Any area included in an official Presidential declaration of a major disaster or emergency. The Department of Homeland Security (DHS) can also identify areas as eligible for Stafford Act preferences.

FAR Part 27, Patents, Data, and Copyrights

FAR Part 27 provides government contracting policy for intellectual property.

How can I become an expert in FAR Part 27?

If you want to become an expert in FAR Part 27, my advice is to abandon your goal. Quit. Do not try. Do not proceed by yourself. Hire an attorney.

How should I proceed when dealing with complicated matters involving intellectual property and government contract law?

Hire a competent attorney specializing in intellectual property *for government contractors*.

Do not hire an attorney who specializes in other areas of the law such as business litigation, family law, or white-collar crime. Do not hire an attorney who specializes in government contract law, but not specifically intellectual property. You need to hire a specialized attorney, someone who focuses on intellectual property *within federal government contract law*.

Intellectual property is vitally important to the survival of your company. Protect your intellectual property by investing in an excellent attorney who specializes in intellectual property within federal government contract law.

FAR Part 28, Bonds and Insurance

FAR Part 28 explains how and when the government requires bonds or insurance.

What does "bid" mean within FAR Part 28, Bonds and Insurance?

Bid means any response to a solicitation, including a proposal or offer. So, your bid is what you send to the government to win a competitive contract.

What is a bid guarantee?

A *bid guarantee* is a form of security assuring that the bidder (1) will not withdraw its bid and (2) will get any required bonds for the contract.

Think of a bid guarantee as an insurance policy that protects the government against the possibility that a bidder will "chicken out" by failing to honor and follow through with its bid. The government needs reassurance that it can rely upon your bid to move forward with the deal. The government also wants assurance that if selected, your company will take all required steps to sign the contract, including obtaining any required bonds.

So, a different company guarantees your company's bid. This different company assures the government of two things. First, your company will not withdraw its bid before the window of time closes for acceptance. Second, your company will follow through with its bid by signing a contract and securing any other bonds required by the government solicitation.

What is a bond?

Let's start with a type of *bond* you may have read about in the news or noticed in a movie about criminals.

If the accused criminal—the defendant—is released after arrest and allowed to go free before the trial, the justice system wants a guarantee that the person will show up for trial. Let's say the judge sets *bail* at $1,000, which means the defendant must pay $1,000 to walk free before the trial.

The *bail bondsman* provides the valuable service of guaranteeing that the person will show up for court. The defendant does not have $1,000 on hand, so the bail bondsman posts the bail bond for the defendant, who pays the bail bondsman ten percent ($100) of the full bond ($1000). The other 90 percent ($900) is covered by *collateral*, such as a house, car, jewelry, or other valuables. So, the bail bondsman pays the bail bond—the full $1,000. The defendant pays 10 percent—just $100—and provides other property or valuables as collateral.

If the defendant shows up to court as promised, the bail bond is dissolved, and the collateral is returned to the owner(s). The bail bondsman keeps the 10 percent ($100) as a service fee.

If the defendant fails to show up, the bail bondsman keeps not just the $100, but also the collateral (the house, car, jewelry, or other valuables that covered the remaining 90 percent or $900).

Can you tell me how this detour into criminal law relates to government contracting?

Back to government contracting and other types of bonds. Your company is like the defendant (sorry!). The government is like the judge. The surety company—which provides the bond for your company—is like the bail bondsman. The government wants assurance that your company will follow through with its obligations to the government, just like the judge wanting assurance that the defendant will keep the promise to show up before the judge in court. In both cases, the *bond* assures fulfillment of promises made by one party to another. In this way, bonds are somewhat like an insurance program because they *share* and *distribute* risk.

The government requires bonds in a variety of situations to limit, mitigate, or eliminate various risks in government contracting, just like the judge requiring bail (or a bail bond) to make sure the defendant shows up in court. When two parties do not trust each other enough, bonds fill in the gap and make the deal go through.

What is a surety company?

The *surety company* provides the bond.

How does the bond, issued by the surety company, protect the government?

The bond is a written instrument (contract) between the surety company and a contractor. The terms of the bond will state that if the contractor fails to fulfill its obligations to the government, the surety company will pay a certain amount of money to compensate the government for its loss. In this way, a bond is somewhat like an insurance policy.

What types of bonds are relevant to government contracting?

Bid bond: This type of bond serves as a bid guarantee, discussed earlier.

Annual bid bond: Instead of executing a series of individual bid bonds, a contractor can provide an annual bid bond that covers all its bids within the same year.

Advance payment bond: Sometimes the government pays a contractor before completing the work. The government wants assurance that the contractor will finish the work (that was already paid for). The advance payment bond covers the cost of the contractor's obligations.

Performance bond: This type of bond provides coverage for the possibility that the contractor fails to complete performance of the contract. Be careful to distinguish a performance bond from a bid bond. The bid bond assures against a bidder failing to honor its bid (before beginning work on the contract). The performance bond assures against a contractor failing to complete its contract (after the contract is signed).

Annual performance bond: Instead of executing a series of individual performance bonds, a contractor can provide an annual performance bond that secures performance for all the contractor's contracts within the same year.

Payment bond: This type of bond assures that the contractor will pay its employees and subcontractors involved in the government contract.

Patent infringement bond: This type of bond secures fulfillment of the contractor's obligations under a patent clause in a contract.

What types of insurance should I explore to protect my company while performing government contracts?

Many! You need to find an excellent insurance broker, agent, or professional to give you insurance advice. Remember, my book is not legal advice, nor is it tax advice, and it is not insurance advice. Contact a qualified professional insurance advisor to meet your insurance needs. This book provides you only the broad strokes to start you on your journey.

As a government contractor, your company probably needs several types of insurance. Even if your company has no government contracts and participates only in the private sector, your company probably needs insurance. Let's explore the different types:

General liability insurance protects against risks like bodily injury or property damage, which are physical, tangible risks. For example, general liability insurance may cover your company for litigation claims if your employee hurts someone else or destroys someone else's computer while performing work. General liability is important for any company, including government contractors.

Professional liability insurance protects against abstract risks like errors or omissions in the services your company provides. For example, professional liability insurance may cover your company for litigation claims if your employees provide inaccurate advice and commit negligence. Just like general liability insurance, professional liability insurance is important for any company providing professional services, including government contractors.

Workers' compensation insurance pays for medical expenses, lost wages, and rehabilitation costs to your employees who become injured or sick at work. Each state has different workers' compensation requirements, but your company is required to pay these costs to employees who get hurt "in the course and scope" of their job. If you have no workers' compensation insurance, your company must pay these costs out-of-pocket. If you have insurance, the insurer pays these costs (in exchange for your monthly premiums). Many states require companies to carry workers' compensation insurance.

FAR PART 29, TAXES

FAR Part 29 is beyond the scope of this book, which does not provide tax advice or legal advice.

How should my company handle the issues presented in FAR Part 29, Taxes?

Hire a tax professional or *Certified Public Accountant (CPA)* for tax advice. Hire an attorney for legal advice. Tax issues are complex and usually involve legal issues as well. Hire a great tax professional for tax questions. Hire a great attorney for legal issues. You may be able to find an attorney who specializes in tax issues—a double threat!

Do you provide tax advice or legal advice?

No. Christoph LLC provides consulting, training, and expert witness services. I can refer you to someone else for tax or legal advice if you email me at **Christoph@ChristophLLC.com**.

FAR Part 30, Cost Accounting Standards Administration

FAR Part 30 describes how and when contractors must follow the Cost Accounting Standards Board rules and regulations.

What is the Cost Accounting Standards Board?

The *Cost Accounting Standards Board (CASB)* was created by Congress to establish cost accounting standards for uniformity and consistency in the measurement, assignment, and allocation of costs for certain government contracts. The CASB established the *Cost Accounting Standards*.

What are the Cost Accounting Standards?

The *Cost Accounting Standards (CAS)* are 19 guidelines or standards created by the CASB specifically for government contracts. If your company wins a CAS-covered government contract, you may be required to follow some or all the Cost Accounting Standards *for that specific contract*.

Are you saying that CAS coverage applies to my entire company?

No, CAS coverage applies on a *contract-by-contract* basis. Companies are not subject to CAS coverage. *Only contracts* may be subject to CAS coverage.

Some, all, or none of your company's government contracts may be subject to CAS coverage. In any case, CAS coverage is applicable to the contract, not to your company. However, your company may need to make companywide changes to accommodate the CAS rules, even though CAS coverage applies on a contract-by-contract basis.

Why is there a set of special Cost Accounting Standards (CAS) only for government contracts instead of using Generally Accepted Accounting Principles (GAAP)?

Great question! I wonder if any lobbyists for the government contracting or accounting industries had anything to do with this situation…

What are some examples of the 19 Cost Accounting Standards?

Accounting for Unallowable Costs
Accounting for Acquisition Costs of Materials
Allocation of Direct and Indirect Costs
Consistency in Allocating Costs Incurred for the Same Purpose

What are CAS-covered contracts?

Contracts that require contractors to follow the Cost Accounting Standards (CAS).

What does full CAS coverage mean?

A contract requiring full CAS coverage must follow all 19 Cost Accounting Standards. Furthermore, your company may need to submit a *disclosure statement* that describes your company's accounting practices.

What does modified CAS coverage mean?

A contract requiring modified CAS coverage must follow only four specific Cost Accounting Standards.

What is the purpose of applying modified CAS coverage versus full CAS coverage?

Think of modified CAS coverage as "dipping your toe in the water." The dollar thresholds and number of CAS-covered government contracts will determine whether your contract(s) require full CAS coverage or modified CAS coverage.

If your company wins a single contract greater than the CAS-coverage dollar threshold, and has no other CAS-covered contracts, you will likely be subject only to modified CAS coverage. In contrast, if your company wins many large contracts, all covered by CAS, you will likely be subject to full CAS coverage. In this way, the government lets your company "ease into" the Cost Accounting Standards.

What types of contracts are subject to CAS coverage?

Generally, cost-reimbursement contracts above a certain dollar threshold are subject to CAS coverage. This rule makes sense because in a cost-reimbursement contract, the government repays your company for any incurred costs which are allowable, allocable, and reasonable. Therefore, the government has a direct interest in how your company keeps track of costs, and the government prefers the Cost Accounting Standards.

What types of contracts are exempt from CAS coverage?

You should learn all the CAS exemptions, but the most common are contracts performed by a small business, contracts using the commercial procedures of FAR Part 12, and contracts under the dollar threshold for submitting certified cost or pricing data.

Are any subcontracts subject to CAS coverage?

Yes, some subcontracts are subject to CAS coverage through requirements imposed by the prime contract.

My subcontract is between my company and the prime contractor—not the government—so how can the government force CAS coverage on my company as a subcontractor?

The government includes a clause in the prime contract requiring the prime contractor to force your company (and any other subcontractors) to adhere to the Cost Accounting Standards in certain situations. In this way, the government "flows down" the CAS coverage requirement through the prime contractor to the subcontractor.

FAR Part 31, Contract Cost Principles and Procedures

FAR Part 31 provides a long list of allowable and unallowable costs.

What is a cost-reimbursement contract?

Read more about cost-reimbursement contracts in FAR Part 16, Types of Contracts.

What are the three considerations for determining whether a cost can be reimbursed?

To determine if a cost is reimbursable (under a cost-reimbursement contract), you need to evaluate three factors: *allowability, allocability,* and *reasonableness*. Ask these three questions: Is this cost allowable? Is this cost properly allocated (to the contract)? Is this cost reasonable?

What is an allowable cost?

Allowability refers to whether that specific cost is explicitly allowed in your contract or in FAR Part 31. You can find a long list of allowable and unallowable costs in FAR Part 31. For example, entertainment costs like season tickets for the regional sports team are unallowable. For another example, the cost of holding shareholders' meetings is allowable.

What if my contract language states a certain cost is unallowable, but that same cost is allowed by FAR Part 31?

In the case of a contradiction between your contract's allowable costs and the rules in FAR Part 31, follow your contract, not FAR Part 31. Sometimes contracting officers will limit or prohibit the allowability of certain costs, even though these same costs are allowable under FAR Part 31. For example, let's say FAR Part 31 allows precontract costs, but your contract specifically excludes precontract costs. In this example, follow your contract.

What is an allocable cost?

Allocable means you can tie the costs or a portion of the costs to the particular contract you are charging the costs against. The cost might be 100% allocable to a single contract—a direct cost. Alternatively, the cost might be spread across several contracts—in other words, an indirect cost.

The good news is the government will reimburse you for both direct and indirect costs. If the cost is indirect (spread across several contracts), you must make sure you attribute ("allocate") an accurate fraction of the cost to the contract you're charging against.

What is a reasonable cost?

Determining whether a cost is *reasonable* is a check mostly used against ridiculous prices or unnecessary expenses. Determining reasonableness is rather subjective, of course.

Who determines whether a cost is reasonable?

The contracting officer decides whether a cost is reasonable or not.

FAR Part 32, Contract Financing

FAR Part 32 explains financing policies for government contracts.

What is the lifeblood of any business?

Cash flow is the lifeblood of any business, including government contractors.

If your company is a federal contractor or subcontractor, you will learn this lesson quickly or go bankrupt slowly. Learn about cash flow.

What is contract financing?

Contract financing consists of different ways to help your company's cash flow by giving you money when you need it so you can perform the contract. There are several types of contract financing.

Are prime contractors required to pay small business subcontractors faster?

Yes, at least sometimes. The federal government's Office of Management and Budget (OMB) released a memo called *"Providing Prompt Payment to Small Business Subcontractors."* This policy memo requires that prime contractors that receive accelerated payment schedules from the government client must also pay small business subcontractors on an accelerated schedule. The idea is that if the prime contractor gets money faster, the prime contractor is supposed to pay any small business subcontractors faster.

What is the Prompt Payment Act?

Congress passed a law requiring agencies to pay contractors within 30 days of submitting a *proper invoice*. Be careful to note that not just any invoice qualifies.

Your company must submit a "proper invoice" by complying with any required format, delivery, or content requirements. Although you may have submitted an invoice 30 days ago, the *Prompt Payment Act* does not start unless your invoice qualifies as a proper invoice. If the agency fails to pay your company within 30 days of a proper invoice, your company receives interest penalties, which discourages the government from dragging its feet.

What are advance payments?

Advance payments are like a special favor to your company. You get payment before you complete the contract. Advance payments are not measured by performance or progress, your company just gets the money early, perhaps to pay subcontractors or for some other reason. Advance payments seem like a great deal but remember that any advance payments will be subtracted from any later payments you are owed. You will not get paid twice for the same work.

What are performance-based payments?

Performance-based payments are based on your company's performance as measured by objective measurements, accomplishment of defined events, or other quantifiable standards or results.

What are progress payments?

Progress payments are based on costs your company incurs during the contract. Progress payments are not based on the percentage or stage of completion, nor are they based on performance, nor are they based on partial delivery. Instead, progress payments are tied to your company's costs (not its results).

What is a "pay when paid" provision and why should I avoid it like the plague?

As a subcontractor, always try to negotiate to remove a *pay when paid* provision. Examine your payment terms and try to decipher if any of the timelines for payment are contingent upon the prime contractor getting paid first. If you need help with this analysis, email me at **Christoph@ChristophLLC.com**.

The subcontractor starts with a cash flow disadvantage. As a subcontractor, you always worry about getting paid on time. First, the prime contractor must be paid by the federal agency. Then, the subcontractor gets paid by the prime contractor. But wait! Is this sequence the only possible order of operation?

Pay when paid provisions between the prime contractor and subcontractor are disturbingly dangerous for the subcontractor. If the prime contractor does not get paid by the federal agency, the subcontractor does not get paid. If the government pays the prime contractor late, the subcontractor's payment is delayed even further.

What are the "Limitation of Funds" and "Limitation of Cost" clauses?

Your cost-reimbursement contract will have a *Limitation of Funds* or *Limitation of Cost* clause that forces you and the contracting officer to closely monitor the cost ceiling. Only the contracting officer has the authority to increase the cost ceiling and obligate more money into the contract. These clauses require your company to give written notice to the government when you approach or know you will surpass the estimated cost ceiling. Read more about these topics in Part 16, Types of Contracts.

FAR Part 33, Protests, Disputes, and Appeals

FAR Part 33 explains how contractors can protest to the agency, GAO, or Court of Federal Claims, and also explains the process for filing a claim under the Contract Disputes Act.

What is the basic difference between filing a claim versus filing a protest?

In short, you file a *claim* during performance of the contract, usually because you want more money. You file a *protest* before performance starts, usually because you lost the contract competition, and you think the government made a mistake.

Can I file a protest about the contract I am currently performing?

No, you have nothing to protest. You won the contract. You're performing the contract. Instead, you could file a *claim*.

Can I file a claim about my competitor winning the contract?

No, because your claim must be based on a contract. You did not win the contract, so you have no contract under which to file a claim. Instead, you could file a *protest*.

Can I ask for more money if circumstances change during contract performance?

Maybe. Before you ask for more money, you need to determine if you are entitled to more money. You need a legitimate reason, not just a sad story about increased costs.

What is the first step to determine whether I can recover more money during contract performance?

The first step is to decide which clause in your contract entitles you to more money. The most common clause mentioned is some form of the *Changes clause*.

What is the Changes clause?

The *Changes clause* allows the government to make unilateral changes to certain parts of the contract. You must comply if the Changes clause is in your contract because that was part of the deal you negotiated. If these changes cost money, then the government must pay you.

What is one way to request more money due to changes in the contract?

You can submit a *request for equitable adjustment (REA),* which is one type of written request for more money due to changes in the contract.

What is another way to request more money due to changes in the contract?

You can submit a *claim,* which is another form of a written request for more money.

How can I learn more about the differences between a claim and REA?

The difference between a claim and REA is complicated. Get a free copy of my full-length article on this topic by emailing **Christoph@ChristophLLC.com**.

What are the basic differences between a claim and REA?

Here are the basics. REAs and claims are two methods for asking for more money on your government contracts. Although REAs and claims are similar, you must understand their important differences. The biggest differences involve the processes after you submit the REA or claim.

Is the REA contract administration or litigation?

REAs are considered contract administration, not litigation. When you submit the REA, you are not taking the first step in suing the government. REAs are not lawsuits. They are considered a normal part of government contract administration. Contract administration costs can be paid by the government.

Can I include the costs of preparing the REA in the REA total cost amount?

Yes. If you hire a consultant like **www.ChristophLLC.com** to help you prepare the REA, you can include your consultant costs in the total amount requested by the REA. In fact, Christoph LLC has successfully written several REAs that got my clients paid, in full, including the Christoph LLC consulting bills. My clients were fully reimbursed by the government for the costs of hiring Christoph LLC for work on the REA, as well as for the underlying basis of the original REA. This tremendous advantage of the REA demonstrates why you should try the REA before the claim.

Does the REA automatically create a deadline for the government to respond?

No. Unfortunately, there is no automatic deadline for the government to respond to your REA. The government can ignore your REA indefinitely. The government could stall, postpone, and delay your REA for months or years. For this reason, you should set firm deadlines for when the government must respond. If you get no response by the deadline, either forward the REA to higher level government officials, or choose to submit a *claim* instead.

Does the claim automatically create a deadline for the government to respond?

Yes. The *claim* starts a process with a deadline requiring a written response from the government, but the REA does not. Unlike REAs, claims force the government contracting officer to respond within a certain time period.

Is filing a claim the first step of potential litigation?

Yes. Claims, unless negotiated and settled, form the basis of adversarial litigation between the government and your company. To encourage settlement, all claims must start with the contracting officer.

Why must all claims start with the contracting officer?

After receiving the claim, the contracting officer must issue your company a *Final Decision*. The Final Decision approves or denies your claim and provides its reasoning.

Can I appeal the Final Decision?

Yes. Once your company receives the Final Decision, you have the option to appeal to either the boards of contract appeals or the United States Court of Federal Claims. In either venue, you can further appeal to the United States Court of Appeals for the Federal Circuit and then to the Supreme Court of the United States.

Can I skip the contracting officer and take my claim directly to the Court of Federal Claims or boards of contract appeals?

No, you cannot take your claim directly to these courts or forums. First, you must submit the claim to the contracting officer and receive the Final Decision. Again, this submission encourages settlement without litigation. You want to get more money for your government contract, and you do not want to spend more money on an expensive lawsuit.

Now, let's return to the topic of the REA.

What is the relationship of the REA to formal litigation?

REAs are considered contract administration, not litigation. REAs should not involve courts or lawsuits.

Ideally, your REA will be resolved quickly and amicably between your company and the contracting officer. Your REA can be resolved by a friendly discussion over the phone that is formalized in a modification to the government contract. Your claim, on the other hand, could turn into a contentious, expensive, and time-consuming legal battle.

Do claims and REAs have different certification requirements?

Yes, claims and REAs have different certification requirements. The confusing part is that both require two identical certifications, but the claim alone also requires two other certifications. This distinction means that REAs must contain two written certifications, while claims require four written certifications.

These certifications should be considered magic words. These words ensure that your REA or your claim will be legitimate and not be rejected. Even more importantly, if you forget the magic words in the four certifications for your claim, then no clock has started ticking. Your claim was *defective*. Forgetting the four certifications means your claim never really occurred and the contracting officer is under no deadline to respond and provide your company a *Final Decision* for the claim. When your company submits a claim or REA, you must make sure you have an expert in government contracting to assist.

Can you summarize the major differences between claims and REAs?

Request for equitable adjustment or REA:

> Considered contract administration
> You can include preparation costs
> Not litigation and not the start of a lawsuit
> Less formal and less aggressive than a claim
> No timeline for the contracting officer to respond

Claim under the Contract Disputes Act:

Considered litigation
  You cannot include preparation costs
  Starts with the contracting officer
  Can result in a lawsuit
  More formal and more aggressive than REA
  Strict time limits for the contracting officer to respond

What is a bid protest?

Generally, a *Government Accountability Office (GAO) bid protest* contests the evaluation and award of a federal contract, or terms of the solicitation. Your proposal was rejected, you lost the contract, and you think you got a raw deal because the government did not follow its own rules. A successful GAO protest can give you a second chance at winning the contract.

Are there other bid protest forums besides the GAO?

Yes, you can also protest to the agency or to the Court of Federal Claims.

What are the important terms and definitions for bid protests?

A bid protest that is decided in favor of your company is *sustained*. If your company loses the bid protest, your bid protest is *denied*.

Some bid protests do not even warrant a full analysis by the GAO. These bid protests are *dismissed* before any serious consideration by the GAO. Being dismissed is much worse than being denied. If your bid protest is dismissed it means your protest was in some way defective. Perhaps your bid protest was untimely because you missed the deadline, resulting in dismissal.

If my GAO bid protest is dismissed or denied, are there other options?

Believe it or not, if the GAO dismisses or denies your bid protest, you can file a nearly identical protest with another forum, the Court of Federal Claims.

Both the GAO and Court of Federal Claims have jurisdiction for bid protests. This dual jurisdiction is very controversial because it allows your company "two bites at the apple." Your company can first try a GAO protest. If that fails, you can try your luck again at the Court of Federal Claims. Just remember that you must start first at the GAO to get "two bites at the apple." If your first bid protest starts at the Court of Federal Claims, you cannot protest afterwards at the GAO. The order of operations is GAO first, then the Court of Federal Claims.

What is the difference between bid protests at the agency, at the GAO, and at the Court of Federal Claims?

There are two main avenues to protest government contract competitions, the GAO and the Court of Federal Claims. You can also protest at the federal agency that conducted the contract competition, but that is usually a waste of time. How likely is it that the same people who rejected your proposal will change their minds when you criticize their ability to do their job correctly? These *agency protests* should only be used if the errors by the federal agency are so obvious that you're confident a higher level federal employee will intervene, fix the problem, and grant your bid protest. Therefore, the two serious avenues for bid protests are the GAO and the Court of Federal Claims, where your company can rely on the opinion of a neutral arbiter, rather than the federal agency itself.

GAO bid protests are faster, cheaper, and simpler than bid protests at the Court of Federal Claims. GAO will usually complete its review of a bid protest within 100 days, while the Court of Federal Claims has no such time limit, often taking much longer to make a decision. The Court of Federal Claims is extremely busy with other litigation involving patents and intellectual property, while the GAO forum focuses exclusively on bid protests.

The Court of Federal Claims follows the Federal Rules of Civil Procedure, which require significantly more legal filings and procedural hurdles. Bid protests at the Court of Federal Claims are slower, more formal, and more expensive. GAO bid protest rules are much simpler, which saves your attorney time and therefore saves your company money.

Can my company protest more than one issue in the same contract competition?

Yes, a bid protest can and probably should allege several different problems with the contract competition, not just one. These individual problems or complaints are often called "counts." Many bid protest attorneys recommend including as many relevant counts as possible because this increases your chance of winning (earning a *sustained* decision).

The government must successfully defend against each and every count of the bid protest. All it takes is one of the counts to succeed for the bid protest to succeed. For this reason, many bid protest attorneys use what is colloquially called the "spaghetti thrown at the wall method." If you throw enough spaghetti at the wall, eventually something will stick. Similarly, if you allege several different counts in your bid protest, you have a better chance of prevailing on at least one of those many counts. Remember, the government needs to defeat every single one of your counts to deny your entire protest. In contrast, all your company needs is one successful count to win (earn a *sustained* bid protest decision). Now you understand why so many attorneys recommend finding as many reasons to protest as possible.

How can a bid protest help my company?

If you win and your bid protest is sustained, your company may have another shot at winning the contract.

While there is no guarantee, it's possible that the government will have to re-evaluate your company's proposal or even restart the entire contract competition, which could result in your company winning the contract. That's the biggest potential advantage of a successful bid protest. While it is rare, some government contractors snatch victory from the jaws of defeat by protesting the award of a government contract to a competitor.

Another advantage derived from bid protests is the right to see more documentation. Lawsuits and bid protests require both parties to disclose or to share relevant documents, so both parties can prepare their arguments and legal briefs. This process of sharing documents with the opposing party is known as *discovery*. During a bid protest, the discovery process may force the government to give your company's attorney new documents or other new information. These new documents or bits of information may strengthen the case for the bid protest or reveal mistakes by the government that require a new contract competition.

For example, your company's attorney may receive the complete explanation for the government decision to award to your competitor. This complete explanation is often called the *source selection decision document*, which reveals the entire reasoning behind why your company lost. This decision document shows how your company and your competitors were rated or evaluated, and how the government valued the relative importance of specific strengths and weaknesses. These insider insights will never cross your attorney's desk unless you protest, because they are considered *source selection sensitive* information. For more information about source selection sensitive information, read Part 3, Improper Business Practices and Personal Conflicts of Interest.

Does it cost money to protest a solicitation or contract award?

Yes, bid protests cost money. The filing fee you pay to the court or GAO is inconsequential—a few hundred dollars. However, your legal bills can cost you more than $100,000. That cost is one reason why clients hire me for an expedited expert opinion, to evaluate their situation, before a fast-talking attorney convinces you to go "all in" and spend big bucks.

Can I save money and file the protest by myself?

Yes, you can protest on your own, without an attorney, a process which is known as *pro se*, but you will get what you pay for.

Can a protest extend the period of performance of my existing contract?

Yes, possibly, but this is a hard-nosed and highly controversial business strategy. Let's say your competitor beat you in the follow-on service contract. Instead of packing your bags and vacating, you can file a bid protest to "freeze" the follow-on award.

If you file a GAO bid protest within certain time limits, you can trigger the *automatic stay* or "freeze" under the Competition in Contracting Act. This "freeze" prevents the government from moving forward with the award to your competitor until the GAO bid protest is resolved.

If the government cannot award the contract to someone else, can you guess who usually gets a contract extension? Yes, your company! Most government contracts have a clause that allows for emergency extensions of as much as 6 months. The GAO bid protest qualifies as an emergency disruption to trigger an emergency extension.

Life is not fair. Protesting to get 6 more months of business and revenue seems underhanded. To be clear, the government client might become very angry. Your competitors will be even angrier — especially those who would have won the next contract if you had not protested. I am not endorsing this practice; I am describing reality.

Should filing a bid protest be my first option when I lose a contract competition?

No, many companies consider bid protests immediately whenever they lose in a contract competition. That's a rookie mistake.

How many GAO bid protests are successful?

Fewer than 5 percent of GAO bid protests are successful.

How do the numbers break down?

Roughly 80 percent of GAO bid protests are "dismissed" at the outset, which means they fail to justify a serious analysis by the GAO. Essentially, these dismissed bid protests fail to make it through the GAO doors. Stated differently, only about one in five or 20 percent of bid protests merit a full decision or recommendation by the GAO.

Of the lucky 20 percent of bid protests that earn a serious analysis from the GAO, roughly 80 percent of those are "denied," meaning the protestor loses and the government wins. These odds are terrible for the protestor. The historical numbers show that four out of five bid protests are dismissed and four out of five of the bid protests that are not dismissed are eventually denied. Is a 4 percent chance worth risking tens of thousands of dollars? Perhaps, if the stakes are high enough.

How can I weigh the pros and cons of filing a protest?

Bid protests are a double-edged sword because they can swing your company fortune in both directions. You might secure a lucrative government contract, or you might ruin your relationship with the government client. The official position is that valid protests serve the process of accountability, but your clients are human and emotional. They may hold grudges. Never forget the human aspect of deciding to protest or not. Government officials may view your protest as a direct insult to their professional competency.

Bid protests are expensive and can ruin relationships. You need to conduct a strategic analysis of your relationships, future pipelines for new work, existing contracts, and other factors to determine your best forward path. Sometimes it is better to spend "exploratory" money to get independent, candid, expert advice…before you file a formal protest.

Be skeptical of trigger-happy bid protest attorneys who recommend a protest. They have a financial incentive to recommend a protest, but that step may not be in your best interest. A few hours of analysis and advice can save you $100,000 down the road. If you want to discuss your unique situation, email me at **Christoph@ChristophLLC.com**.

FAR Part 34, Major System Acquisition

FAR Part 34 provides limited directions for acquiring major systems.

What does "major systems" mean?

Large, grand, complex, expensive — measured in the millions or billions of dollars. The Department of Defense uses terms like *"Major Defense Acquisition Program" (MDAP)* to describe its biggest contracts.

Do I need a team of lobbyists?

If your company delivers products or services related to major systems, measured in the millions or billions of dollars, you should consider hiring a team of lobbyists to influence Congress. Why? Because all your major competitors already have lobbyists in Washington, DC.

I am not endorsing, praising, or condoning the system that all but requires lobbyists. I am merely informing you about the reality of the American defense and contracting industry. President Eisenhower called it the "military-industrial complex" in his farewell address in 1961.

Do you think Lockheed Martin hires lobbyists? Do you think Boeing hires lobbyists? They do. Why do you think Amazon opened an office right outside of Washington, DC? Again, I am not endorsing, praising, or condoning this system. I am describing real conditions and events on planet Earth, the United States of America.

What do federal contractors need to know about FAR Part 34, Major System Acquisition?

Not much, spend your valuable time elsewhere.

Why do you say so?

I worked as a federal employee (contract specialist) for the *Air Force Space Command, Space and Missile Systems Center*, specializing in major, space-based weapons systems, measured in the billions of dollars. Think of satellites, rockets, global positioning systems. FAR Part 34 (Major System Acquisition) was not important to my on-the-job education or experience. If you read through FAR Part 34 and find something to blow my hair back and knock my socks off, please email me at **Christoph@ChristophLLC.com**.

FAR PART 35, RESEARCH AND DEVELOPMENT CONTRACTING

FAR Part 35 provides special contracting procedures for research and development, including Broad Agency Announcements with peer or scientific review.

What is the primary purpose of research and development contracting?

The primary purpose of *research and development contracting* is to advance scientific and technical knowledge, which is an abstract goal. Other types of contracting have concrete goals, such as delivering 2,000 pounds of crude oil or mowing 100 square miles of grass on an Army base.

Research and development contracts have abstract goals that cannot be described in advance, in contrast to supplies and services, which can be defined clearly. The government cannot predict the future, nor can it predict which research programs will succeed or fail. Therefore, research and development contracting encourages the top minds in science, technology, and industry to submit unique, creative proposals, usually through the Broad Agency Announcement process. The government uses experts in the same fields to judge the technical merits of these proposals with the lofty goal of advancing the state of the art.

What is a Broad Agency Announcement?

Broad Agency Announcements (BAA) are used to announce the government's interest in one or more research topics. BAAs should only be used when the government expects meaningful proposals with varying technical or scientific approaches. In other words, the government does not know what it wants, other than to explore new frontiers of science or technology.

Why are research BAAs so different from traditional government contracting?

Remember this phrase: "No common Statement of Work."

When using BAAs, the government expects a wide variety of possible research programs, which is different from most government contracting competitions. In most competitions, each company competes to provide the best solution for the same Statement of Work. In a BAA competition, every company submits a different research idea making it nearly impossible to compare the proposals against one another sensibly. When contracting for research, there is no common Statement of Work.

Why must BAAs request general topics for research rather than specific goods or services?

The BAA process is a special procurement method for exploring new areas of research, not for buying things like supplies or services that the government can adequately describe. If the agency needs a specific system or hardware solution, then BAAs are not appropriate and the agency should use other methods of competitive contracting.

What are the four requirements of a BAA?

The BAA must describe the agency's research interest(s), so that industry understands the broad topics of the BAA. The method of evaluation, including the criteria for selection and their relative importance, must be described in the BAA. The government must specify the period during which proposals will be accepted. Finally, the BAA must contain instructions for preparing and submitting proposals. Therefore, the BAA must answer the following questions:

What is the research topic?
How will proposals be evaluated?
When can proposals be submitted and accepted?
What must proposals contain and how must they be submitted?

How are BAA proposals evaluated?

BAA proposals are evaluated using either peer or scientific review.

What is peer or scientific review?

Peer or scientific review is a group of experts evaluating proposals from BAAs. These experts should be qualified within the field(s) of expertise related to the proposal topic. For example, if the BAA calls for proposals for cancer research, the group of experts may consist of cancer research scientists and medical doctors specializing in cancer (oncologists). If the BAA asks for research proposals about artificial intelligence, the group of experts may consist of mathematicians and computer scientists.

Is price important in a BAA for research?

Price is not really important, and this difference distinguishes the BAA process from almost every other competitive process in the FAR. Since BAAs are designed to get the best research available from cutting-edge scientists, research institutions, and technology companies, other factors overshadow price. Although the agency will evaluate your cost and price, those details will not be the primary basis for selection.

What factors do agencies use to select proposals from BAAs?

Proposal selection decisions are based on the following factors: technical, importance to agency programs, and "funding availability."

What does "funding availability" mean?

Usually, the government has a fixed budget to spend on the research area(s) and topic(s) covered by the BAA. The government selects the best proposals until it runs out of money. So, *funding availability* just means the government has money remaining in the budget to fund the research project. Funding availability should be distinguished from concepts like "getting the lowest price" or "tradeoffs between price and technical factors."

What do "technical" and "importance to agency programs" mean?

These factors indicate how much discretion agencies have in the evaluation and selection of proposals under research BAAs. *Technical* is a broad and subjective term to describe the research merits of the proposal. Since research, by definition, explores possibilities that do not yet exist, evaluating proposals based on their technical merit calls for quite a bit of discretion. The agency's peer or scientific review team will decide whether your proposal's "technical" merit deserves the award. *Importance to agency programs* simply describes how well your research proposal lines up with the goals of the agency and its research program(s).

Can agencies award other instruments from BAAs, like grants?

Yes, BAAs often allow funding of FAR-based procurement contracts, assistance instruments like grants and cooperative agreements, and even "Other Transactions," a special type of government contract for research or prototypes (and sometimes full manufacturing production from the prototypes).

What are grants, cooperative agreements, and Other Transactions?

Grants are appropriate when the research topic stimulates an area that benefits public policy, such as cancer research, but the government needs little to no involvement in the process. If you receive a grant, your company may receive money with little expected in return other than a final report of research results. *Cooperative agreements* are much like grants — stimulating research rather than obtaining direct benefits or deliveries — yet cooperative agreements allow greater government involvement in the research process.

Other Transactions use a special authority that allows the government to craft flexible contracts for research or prototypes, with almost as much leeway as a private-sector contract, unburdened from most of the laws, regulations, and policy shackles that handcuff traditional government contracts. One policy goal of Other Transactions is to attract nontraditional, innovative companies that otherwise avoid government contracts because of restrictive regulations like the FAR, grasping intellectual property clauses, or complicated Cost Accounting Standards. Any BAA should specify exactly which types of government contracts or agreements it intends to award, such as FAR-based procurement contracts, grants, cooperative agreements, and Other Transactions.

FAR Part 36, Construction and Architect-Engineer Contracts

FAR Part 36 provides contracting procedures for the special fields of construction, architecture, engineering, and related services.

Why is construction contracting different?

Construction *creates* a building or other structure, possibly from the ground up. So many things can go wrong: accidents, delays, shady subcontractors, weather problems, structural collapses, and unforeseen conditions. With so many different steps in the construction process — excavation, foundation, concrete, drywall, insulation, masonry — construction involves an exceptionally long chain of subcontractors, and "subcontractors to the subcontractors." Construction involves many points of failure and catastrophic failure can literally kill people.

Government contracts for construction use special clauses to mitigate these risks, such as clauses for site inspection, subcontracting, liquidated damages, workmanship, permits, accident prevention, and cleaning up. You will not encounter these special construction clauses in the performance of government contracts for supplies, services, or research and development. Construction is a special breed.

What are architect-engineer services?

Architect-engineer (A-E) services include professional services required by state law to be performed by licensed architects or engineers, such as the design or construction of real estate property. A-E services can also include incidental services like surveying property boundaries, performing studies, mapping, or soil engineering.

Why is A-E contracting different?

Congress passed a law called the *Brooks Act* that mandates a special *qualifications-based selection* of government contractors for A-E services. Contractors are selected primarily on competence and qualifications, with the negotiation of price coming a distant second. First, the government selects the highest rated contractor, then negotiates a reasonable price. If the second step fails to produce a reasonable price or a signed contract, the government moves to the second-best choice, and so forth.

The policy justification for A-E contracting is that you must "get it right the first time" by hiring qualified professionals, rather than saving money with a cheap, unqualified contractor that causes a building to collapse or creates a million-dollar lawsuit by performing the boundary survey wrong. Focusing on qualifications and competence makes sense when you consider the dire consequences of hiring inferior professionals for these A-E services.

FAR Part 37, Service Contracting

FAR Part 37 encourages performance-based acquisition and provides contracting policy for service contracts.

What is a service contract?

A service contract pays for a contractor to perform a task, rather than to supply an item. For example, cleaning a toilet, analyzing the FAR, and collecting garbage are all services.

What is the government's preferred method for acquiring services?

The government encourages the use of performance-based acquisition for service contracts. Architect-engineering, construction, and utility services represent exceptions to this rule and do not require performance-based acquisition.

What is performance-based acquisition?

Performance-based acquisition uses a *Performance Work Statement (PWS)* instead of a Statement of Work (SOW), measurable performance standards, and a method of measuring contractor performance against these objective standards.

The goal of performance-based acquisition is to save money and achieve better results by using commercial solutions. Instead of telling the experts in industry how to perform services, ask for the desired outcome and let the contractor impress the client with its ingenuity.

What is the difference between a PWS and SOW?

A *Performance Work Statement (PWS)* describes measurable performance standards (quality, timeliness, quantity) and focuses on the desired outcome. In contrast, a Statement of Work (SOW) provides detailed instructions for how to perform the work.

For example, a SOW might state that "the contractor shall use a gas-powered lawn mower, three times per month, during daylight hours to mow the grass on the Army base." In contrast, a PWS might state that "the contractor shall keep the grass on the Army base between three and five inches in height at all times." The SOW dictates exactly how the contractor will cut the grass, while the PWS lets the contractor figure out the most sensible way to achieve the desired result.

This example PWS has measurable performance standards: the height of the grass should be always between three and five inches. In this example, the government's method of measuring the contractor's performance might be a "spot check" once per week with measuring tape.

Is the difference between a PWS and SOW sometimes illusory, and merely "form over substance?"

Yes, unfortunately. In the real world, sometimes the government employee literally deletes the title of "Statement of Work" and substitutes "Performance Work Statement," with no substantive differences whatsoever. This so-called "PWS" describes exactly how your company must perform the work, rather than describing the desired results. When this tomfoolery happens, we have a classic case of form over substance. The document has a new title (PWS) but nothing changed. You may encounter a so-called "PWS" that is merely a SOW in disguise.

How does the government measure whether the contractor meets performance standards of a PWS?

One common method for measuring the contractor's adherence to the performance standards of a PWS is called a *Quality Assurance Surveillance Plan* or *QASP* (rhymes with "wasp").

Sometimes the government designs the QASP and sometimes the government requires the contractor to design the QASP. Either way, the QASP will be a critical document to measure your success under the government contract. Become familiar with the QASP, which will describe exactly how and when the government will "checkup" on your performance.

What are personal services?

In government contracting, *personal services* refers to a contract that creates an employer-employee relationship. Of course, hiring "contractors" is designed specifically to avoid creating an employer-employee relationship. The government employee is supposed to hire a contractor to perform a contract, wherein the contractor uses its own employees. In this way, the government maintains a contractual relationship with its contractor, and does not create an employer-employee relationship.

Why does the government avoid creating personal services contracts?

I will tell you a secret. The secret reason is that if a government contractor performs personal services, the government may be liable for benefits owed to employees, such as overtime, health care, and pensions. You may have heard that federal employees have extraordinary benefits when compared to the private sector. The government fears the possibility of a government contractor successfully suing the government for a lump-sum payment representing these benefits.

I have questions about my contract or proposal involving services, can you help me?

Maybe. Email me at **Christoph@ChristophLLC.com**.

FAR Part 38, Federal Supply Schedule Contracting

FAR Part 38 explains government policy for using the GSA Schedules Program.

What do federal contractors need to know about FAR Part 38, Federal Supply Schedule Contracting?

Not much. FAR Part 38 is short, more relevant for the government, and not useful for federal contractors. Spend your valuable time elsewhere.

If you want to learn more about GSA Schedule contracts (which is the same thing as the Federal Supply Schedule or FSS), read Part 8, Required Sources of Supplies and Services.

FAR Part 39, Acquisition of Information Technology

FAR Part 39 covers special issues in contracting for information technology.

What do federal contractors need to know about FAR Part 39, Acquisition of Information Technology?

Not much. Spend your valuable time elsewhere, but make sure you read my answer to the final question in this chapter.

What do federal contractors—specializing in information technology—need to know about FAR Part 39?

Not much. Read through it to understand the special requirements for providing *information technology (IT) services* to the government. You will read references to OMB Circular A-130 (Management of Federal Information Resources), OMB Circular A-127 (Financial Management Systems), and Section 508 of the Rehabilitation Act.

I'll share my experience, which may differ from others. I was a federal employee (contract specialist) and I was involved in millions of dollars of IT contracts. I was also the government contracts expert for a defense contractor that specialized in IT services, among other things. In my experience, FAR Part 39 was not important or helpful in either position.

If FAR Part 39 is not helpful, what advice do you have for federal IT contractors?

Know your client. Learn and understand as much as you can about the mission of the federal agency client. Try to conceptualize the operational constraints of the employees who work for that agency. Clients will trust your company and its products and services if you demonstrate a commitment to understanding the agency.

Be extremely careful with "scope creep," which is a colloquial phrase for when the government's requirements expand beyond what was written or contemplated in the contract. For example, during performance of your contract, the government realizes it wants much more than what is required by the statement of work. Understand your statement of work and its limitations. Do not work for free but do not upset the client.

Manage your client's expectations. Do not promise or agree to unrealistic requests. Walk your client "away from the cliff." Do not be afraid to say, "We cannot do that for the following reasons." However, you should offer an alternative solution that solves the problem. Avoid handing complete control of your project schedule to the government client. Watch your deadlines and deliverables.

If your company is asked to perform work that is not required by the contract, think very carefully about performing that work "for free." Do not be afraid to respectfully push back on any request to perform work that is outside the scope of the contract. Ask for a written contract modification to change the statement of work, which will entitle your company to an "equitable adjustment" (more money to pay for the new work).

If you provide onsite IT support for a federal client, train your employees to observe the working environment to better understand the client. Having "boots on the ground" is invaluable intelligence to help you better serve your client. Listen to your line-level employees and ask them what problems they see at the agency. Those problems can be solved by your company, perhaps winning you more contracts and greater client trust.

You might know much more about IT than your government client, but do not rub it in anyone's face. Be professional, be patient, and never be arrogant or condescending. The government outsources most of its IT knowledge, which means it hires smart contractors to do the heavy lifting. You can be that smart contractor, but nobody will like you (or hire you) if you come across as unpleasant. Be kind, be courteous, be humble.

If you sell software, consider *how* you will sell it. Will you sell software licenses? Will the license be for the entire agency's use? One license per office? One license per person? Will your license be subscription-based, with annual renewals? Will your license be a one-time payment? Will you require upgrade costs? What about maintenance? Can your company offer tailored solutions as the agency's needs change? Will your company offer a team of onsite support specialists to complement the software licenses, thereby expanding your software company into the services industry? Think through these and other questions carefully—they will make or break your company's fortune as a federal IT contractor. If you need more help, email me at **Christoph@ChristophLLC.com**.

FAR Part 40, Reserved

FAR Part 40 is reserved. Nothing to see here! FAR Part 40 has no text because it is reserved for future use.

Check out my online courses available at **Courses.ChristophLLC.com**.

Have you read my first book, the bestselling <u>Government Contracts in Plain English</u>? Get your copy at **https://www.amazon.com/dp/173419815X/**

You should also read my third book, <u>Government Contracts Negotiation, Simplified</u>! Buy your copy at **https://www.amazon.com/dp/1734198133**

Buy all the books in *The Government Contracts in Plain English Series*, available at **https://www.amazon.com/dp/B09MRCMWBD?binding=paperback**

When you need my help, email me at **Christoph@ChristophLLC.com**

FAR Part 41, Acquisition of Utility Services

FAR Part 41 is relevant only for utility companies.

What do federal contractors need to know about FAR Part 41, Acquisition of Utility Services?

Not much. FAR Part 41 provides instructions to the government to acquire utility services. Unless you own or work for a utility company, spend your valuable time elsewhere.

FAR Part 42, Contract Administration and Audit Services

FAR Part 42 explains how the government may assign certain contract administration and audit tasks to other personnel or agencies.

Can the contracting officer delegate contract administration responsibilities?

Yes, under certain contracts, such as complex, cost-reimbursement contracts, the contracting officer may delegate several responsibilities to the *administrative contracting officer (ACO)*. The procurement contracting officer or PCO signed the contract, the ACO may later administer many aspects of the contract. The PCO may delegate administrative powers to an ACO who works for a different federal agency, such as the *Defense Contract Management Agency (DCMA)*.

What types of functions might the ACO perform?

The ACO may be involved in many activities with your company, especially on complex, cost-reimbursement contracts. These functions may include:

Negotiating forward pricing rate agreements (FPRA)
Negotiating advance agreements for contract costs
Determining whether to allow reimbursement of specific costs
Establishing final indirect cost rates or billing rates
Determining the adequacy of your company's accounting system
Processing any formal name changes of your company
Approving your company's subcontracts

Can the contracting officer delegate contract audit responsibilities?

Yes, contracting officers may delegate audit responsibilities to other agencies that special in such audits, such as the *Defense Contract Audit Agency (DCAA)*, which is tasked with performing all contract audits for the Department of Defense.

FAR Part 43, Contract Modifications

FAR Part 43 explains the various types of contract modifications you may encounter.

What is a unilateral modification?

A *unilateral modification* changes the terms and conditions of your contract but requires no signature from the contractor. Therefore, the contracting officer issues the modification *unilaterally*.

What is a bilateral modification?

A *bilateral modification* changes the terms and conditions of your contract using a signature from both the contracting officer and contractor. Another term for bilateral modification is *supplemental agreement*.

What is an administrative change or administrative modification?

An *administrative change* or *administrative modification* is a type of unilateral modification that does not affect the rights or obligations of the contractor. For example, the contracting officer may change the type of appropriated money used to pay you, or may change the government payment office that sends you money, but there is no effect on your payments or rights.

Can a unilateral modification change my obligations under the contract?

Yes, for example, a unilateral modification under the *Changes clause* requires your company to comply. Although your company may be entitled to an *equitable adjustment* (more money), you are obligated to follow the directions of any proper exercise of the Changes clause. Another example is a unilateral *exercise of an option*: Your company has no choice but to perform the option period if it is properly exercised in a unilateral modification.

How can I distinguish between unilateral and bilateral modifications?

Always look at Block 13 of the *Standard Form (SF) 30*, which describes the contracting officer's authority or justification for issuing the modification.

What is the Changes clause?

Several versions of the *Changes clause* allow the government to change the contract unilaterally, within certain limits, using a change order. Your company must comply with authorized changes, although you may be entitled to an *equitable adjustment*. For more info, read Part 33, Protests, Disputes, and Appeals, as well as Part 52, Solicitation Provisions and Contract Clauses.

What is a change order?

A *change order* is any form of written direction from the contracting officer that requires your company to perform the contract differently. The change order can be a formal modification or an email or a letter. Based on the *Changes clause*, the contracting officer directs some change and your company must comply. However, your company may be entitled to an *equitable adjustment* (more money, a schedule extension, or some other relief).

Do commercial government contracts allow for unilateral change orders?

No, commercial government contracts using FAR Part 12 procedures do not allow for unilateral changes. All changes under commercial government contracts must be agreed upon by signature of the contracting officer and contractor. If your commercial government contract includes some version of the Changes clause, you should negotiate to remove it. For more info about commercial contracting procedures, read Part 12, Acquisition of Commercial Items.

What is a constructive change?

A *constructive change* is a doctrine of law invented by judges that protects your company from getting "ripped off." If the contracting officer's words, writings, communications, acts, or failure to act causes your company to make changes under the contract—even though there was no formal change order—the *doctrine of constructive changes* may entitle your company to an equitable adjustment. In other words, if the contracting officer's action or inaction seems like a change order—even though it was not a formal, written change order—it may be construed or interpreted as if it were a formal, written change order.

This doctrine protects your company from being swindled by a contracting officer who nudges you towards different work and refuses to pay you because "there was no official, written change order." Be careful about relying on constructive changes. A better idea is to ask for a written modification whenever you suspect a change order or any change to the contract.

What is an equitable adjustment?

An *equitable adjustment* is a modification to the contract price, schedule, or other terms to reflect changed circumstances. Most equitable adjustments are in response to a change order directed by the contracting officer under the Changes clause. For example:

1. Contracting officer issues a change order to use more expensive material
2. Your company complies with the change order because of the Changes clause
3. Your company incurs greater costs than contemplated under the original contract
4. Your company submits a request for equitable adjustment (REA) for more money
5. Contracting officer grants your REA
6. Contracting officer modifies the contract to pay you more money (equitable adjustment)

What is a request for equitable adjustment or REA?

Learn more about *requests for equitable adjustment (REA)* and *claims* under the Contract Disputes Act in Part 33, Protests, Disputes, and Appeals. You can also read my full-length article on this topic by emailing me at **Christoph@ChristophLLC.com**.

If a modification is described as "no big deal," why should my company take a closer look?

Sometimes the government contracting officer will include changes or updates to clauses in the contract. "No big deal," the contracting officer may say. "These are just the latest versions of the same clauses."

Do not fall for this dirty trick. Yes, of course, the Federal Acquisition Regulation (FAR) clauses change over time. Yes, it is true that each FAR clause shows the timing of the last update or version of that clause—for example, November 2016. None of this information is relevant to your specific contract. Your specific contract was a deal you struck, precisely showing all the clauses in your contract, as of the date of the contract.

If the government wants to change or update any of these clauses, your company may be entitled to receive more money or some other *consideration*. When you hear the term *consideration*, think of money or something else of recognizable value.

What is a Contractor's Statement of Release?

Sometimes the modification will include language that waives your right to request money or other relief to comply with the new clauses. Watch out for this language in your modification:

> "Contractor's Statement of Release
> In consideration of the modification(s) agreed to herein as complete equitable adjustments for the Contractor's _____ (describe) _____ "proposal(s) for adjustment," the Contractor hereby releases the Government from any and all liability under this contract for further equitable adjustments attributable to such facts or circumstances giving rise to the "proposal(s) for adjustment" (except for_____)."

You might sign this modification, eager to proceed, but not recognizing that you are also signing away your rights to additional money. Do not make this mistake. Review every modification carefully, even if it's "no big deal."

Should I permit any changes to the contract that are not formalized in writing?

No! Do not allow the government to make changes to your business relationship that are not established in writing. The change can start off with a conversation, but it must be followed by something in writing. I have seen countless disasters that could have been avoided by following this advice.

FAR Part 44, Subcontracting Policies and Procedures

FAR Part 44 explains when the government may require approval of your subcontracting decisions, and also covers the Contractor Purchasing System Review process.

I thought subcontracting is between my company and its subcontractors, and therefore none of the government's business. Are you saying the government must approve all my subcontracting decisions?

Not exactly. Check your contract for *FAR clause 52.244-2, Subcontracts*. The answer depends on the type of government contract and whether your company has an approved purchasing system. For most fixed-price contracts, you do not need government approval for your subcontracts. For many cost-reimbursement contracts, and for many time and materials contracts, it gets significantly more complicated *if your contract includes FAR clause 52.244-2, Subcontracts…*

If your company has an approved purchasing system, you need government approval for only the subcontracts specifically identified in the contract. In such cases, the contracting officer will list subcontracts or categories thereof that require government approval.

If your company does not have an approved purchasing system, you need government approval for subcontracts that are cost-reimbursement or time-and-materials, or that are fixed-price yet represent five percent or more of the total estimated value of the *prime contract*.

Note: For the special category of fixed-price subcontracts that require consent, there are two different dollar value thresholds for two sets of federal agencies, so actually, five percent of the prime contract value is not the only threshold.

For the Department of Defense, the Coast Guard, and the National Aeronautics and Space Administration, the threshold is the *greater of* the simplified acquisition threshold or five percent. For other federal agencies, the dollar value threshold is *either* the simplified acquisition threshold or five percent. Run the numbers in your head and you will find that it is more practicable to simply explain the threshold of five percent.

Do I need consent to subcontract for my commercial prime contracts?

No, the FAR provides an exception to the consent-to-subcontract requirement for commercial prime contracts that use FAR Part 12 procedures (so-called "commercial government contracts"). For more info, read Part 12, Acquisition of Commercial Items.

Can my company receive advance approval for certain subcontracts?

Yes, if you know your company will be subject to FAR clause 52.244-2, Subcontracts, you should ask the contracting officer to provide advance approval by listing your expected subcontracts in that clause. Save time by planning ahead!

What is an approved purchasing system?

An *approved purchasing system* refers to your company's subcontracting (purchasing) processes, policies, and procedures. If the government has formally reviewed and approved your company's subcontracting operations, then your company has an approved purchasing system. If your company fails this test, or has never been subject to a review, then your company does not have an approved purchasing system.

What is the name for the process whereby the government reviews, evaluates, and (hopefully) approves my company's purchasing system?

Contractor purchasing system review (CPSR) refers to a complete evaluation — by the government — of your company's subcontracting and purchasing process, including how your company selects and manages subcontractors.

How important is the success or failure of my company's CPSR?

A successful CPSR is vitally important to the future of your company as a government contractor. If you expect a CPSR soon, you should invest time and money to prepare your company to be approved. Do not try to figure this process out by yourself.

Hire experienced accountants and compliance experts *who specialize in government contracting and CPSRs*. Search for experts who have participated in successful (approved) CPSRs. Be careful with accountants who say they can help you with a CPSR but have never actually been through a successful CPSR. You need an experienced specialist with proven success.

What happens if my company fails a CPSR?

If you fail a CPSR, your priority is to immediately improve your operations to succeed in the next CPSR. Without an approved purchasing system, your company is at a competitive disadvantage for many types of contracts. Remember, an approved purchasing system means your company can skip most of the subcontracting approval process.

What will the government examine during a CPSR?

The CPSR will pay special attention to the following factors in your company's operational policy for awarding subcontracts:

Market research
Price competition
Pricing policy, such as requesting certified cost or pricing data
Evaluation of subcontractor responsibility, such as checking SAM.gov
Policies related to encouraging small business participation as a subcontractor
Planning, award, and post-award management of larger subcontracts
Compliance with Cost Accounting Standards (CAS) rules
Selecting the appropriate payment arrangement for subcontracts
Management internal controls
Periodic self-assessments or self-audits of your company's subcontracting operations

Who will provide or withhold subcontracting approval?

The contracting officer provides approval to subcontract. There are different types of contracting officers.

The *procurement contracting officer (PCO)* is the contracting officer who negotiated and signed your contract. Sometimes the PCO will delegate administrative duties to an *administrative contracting officer (ACO)*. In that case, the ACO is responsible for providing consent to subcontract. If the PCO retained this duty and did not delegate it to the ACO, the PCO is responsible for providing consent to subcontract. In either situation, it will be a contracting officer who gives your company permission to subcontract, if required.

Should I position my company as a prime contractor or subcontractor?

With few exceptions, prime contractors get better profit margins and closer relationships with the government client. Prime contractors also bear the full responsibility for the contract, even if subcontractors fail.

Subcontractors give up workshare and profit margins, but they get to work on smaller contracts and avoid having a direct contract with the government, a condition that has significant advantages. Many government contracting companies start with subcontracts to gain experience and confidence, and then pursue prime contracts later.

What is a prime contractor?

Government contracts are often performed by several different companies in a cascading pattern. The first contractor wins a government contract. The first contractor is known as the *prime contractor*.

What is a subcontractor?

The prime contractor cannot or does not want to perform 100 percent of the work, so the prime contractor finds a second contractor to perform a portion of the work. The second contractor is known as the *subcontractor*.

When the first contractor (prime contractor) and second contractor (subcontractor) sign a contract to perform some of the work — a portion of the original government prime contract — that is called a *subcontract*.

Is "subcontract" a relative term?

Yes, the term "subcontract" is always relative to the original contract with the government. The subcontractor, of course, can also subcontract a portion of its work to other companies. "Subcontract of a subcontract" sounds awkward, so you call it a 2nd-tier subcontract performed by a 2nd-tier subcontractor.

The 2nd-tier subcontractor, of course, can also subcontract a portion of its work to a 3rd-tier subcontractor, and so forth. The various "tiers" or "levels" of subcontracting indicate the distance from the original government contract, which is a contract between the government and the prime contractor.

Why should I beware the "telephone game?"

The farther away your company is from the prime contract with the government, the more complicated the business relationship. Just like the "telephone game" that children play, the original message from the government is likely to change as it passes from prime contractor to subcontractor to 2nd-tier subcontractor. Beware this phenomenon.

Should I be skeptical of hearsay?

Yes, you should be skeptical of hearsay, which is information received from someone other than the alleged source of the statement, and which you cannot verify.

For example, the prime contractor tells you, the subcontractor, that the government wants you, the subcontractor, to do something. You can consider that hearsay until you verify the government made the request.

Always be skeptical when your prime contractor describes messages that allegedly came from the government. There is a very good chance that the original message from the government was distorted or changed by one of the middlemen. Any distortion is likeliest to benefit the prime contractor, and not your subcontracting company. Be skeptical!

What is "privity of contract?"

Only the prime contractor has a direct contractual relationship with the government client. This direct contractual relationship is called *privity of contract* — an important concept to understand. If you have a contract with another party, then you have "privity of contract" with that other party. The two of you share a relationship in that you are both parties to a single contract that applies to both of you.

Do subcontractors have privity of contract with the government?

The prime contractor has privity of contract with the government. The prime contractor also has privity of contract with the subcontractor. However, the subcontractor does not have privity of contract with the government. The subcontractor only has a direct contractual relationship with the prime contractor, in the form of a subcontract. You must understand this dynamic.

Who bears all the risk of failure under a government contract — the prime contractor or subcontractor?

Although a subcontractor may also support the government client, there is only one prime contractor. The risk of failure for the entire government contract belongs to the prime contractor, not the subcontractor. As a prime contractor, blaming a subcontractor, even if the subcontractor fails, is simply not an option. The prime contractor bears all the risk and responsibility for its entire chain of subcontracts.

What are the advantages of being the prime contractor?

With greater risk comes greater rewards. Prime contractors have several advantages over subcontractors. Your cash flow is better because you get paid first. Imagine being a 3rd-tier subcontractor. The 3rd-tier subcontractor waits for the prime contractor to get paid, then the subcontractor, then the 2nd-tier subcontractor. You're lucky if each stage takes only 30 days. That's why the negotiation of payment terms is so important.

Not only is the prime contractor paid first, it also gets the lion's share of the profits. Any subcontractor is negotiating for a subset or fraction of the entire profit of the government contract — whatever the prime contractor is willing to subcontract away. Profit margins for lower tier subcontractors usually get smaller and smaller as each middleman takes a cut.

Prime contractors are closer to the government client. The United States of America is the largest client in world history. It pays to work with a client that spends more than a trillion dollars every year in government contracts and grants. Your book of business can grow as contact with one federal agency leads to new work or new clients at other federal agencies.

What are the advantages of being a subcontractor?

Maybe you don't want to do business with the government. Remember, a subcontractor does not have "privity of contract" or a direct contractual relationship with the government. That lack of a direct contractual relationship can be a significant advantage.

As a subcontractor, you have a contract simply with another private business. If you have problems or litigation, you are subject to private sector contract law rather than federal contract law. As a professor and expert witness in federal contract law, I can assure you that several aspects of federal contract law favor the government and not the contractors.

Subcontractors can avoid most of the aspects of federal contract law that heavily favor the government. A subcontract between two businesses will be subject to the same legal conventions as any other private sector contract. Litigation between two subcontractors (or between a prime contractor and subcontractor) will often take place in state court, rather than federal court. In contrast, contract litigation between a prime contractor and the federal government will be subject to federal contract law, and will likely take place in federal court.

Subcontracts have greater freedom to design and negotiate contract terms. Government contracts with the prime contractor are bound by strict regulations like the Federal Acquisition Regulation (FAR), but subcontracts have more flexibility. Take advantage of this flexibility whenever possible. Negotiate terms that protect you as a subcontractor.

Your negotiating position will likely be weak in relation to the prime contractor or a higher tier subcontractor. Do not let the prime contractor push you into an unfavorable subcontract. Be prepared to walk away, if necessary. Another advantage of being a subcontractor is the reserved power to choose your contracts carefully, and to walk away from unwise opportunities or shady business partners.

Subcontractors can get a foot in the door by performing smaller portions of government contracts without shouldering all the risk and responsibility. Subcontractors can target new types of work and gain valuable experience and contacts while avoiding the crushing possibility of failure in front of the government client. In this way, subcontractors can practice in the minor leagues (subcontracts with other companies) before stepping up to the major leagues (prime contracts with the government).

FAR Part 45, Government Property

FAR Part 45 explains the contractor's responsibility for handling government property, such as Government Furnished Property and Contractor Acquired Property.

What is government property?

Government property is any property owned or leased by the government.

What is the overall policy for government property versus contractor property?

Generally, the contractor should furnish all property needed to perform the government contract. Contracting officers *may*, at their discretion, provide your company government property to use during the contract.

What are the two most important types of government property for government contracts?

Government Furnished Property (GFP) and *Contractor Acquired Property (CAP)*.

What is GFP and what is CAP?

Government Furnished Property (GFP) is possessed or acquired *by the government* and furnished to the contractor for performance of the contract. *Contractor Acquired Property (CAP)* is *purchased or fabricated by the contractor* for use in the contract, but the government retains title (ownership) and has not yet received and accepted the property. CAP is usually encountered under cost-reimbursement or time-and-material contracts.

For example, if the government gives your company a special entry badge to swipe into the building doors, that is GFP. If your company fabricates a special weapon during a cost-reimbursement contract, and the government will receive and accept that weapon under the contract, that is likely CAP. Both GFP and CAP are types of *government property*. Both these examples—the badge and weapon—are owned by the government, although they are *possessed* by the contractor during performance.

Does my company have a responsibility to keep track of GFP, CAP, and government property under the contract?

Yes, check your contract for any government property clause(s), which may require you to control, use, preserve, protect, repair, track, organize, account, or deliver these items.

FAR Part 46, Quality Assurance

FAR Part 46 explains how the government will verify that your performance or delivery meets the quality standards of your government contract.

What does acceptance mean within the context of FAR Part 46, Quality Assurance?

Acceptance is when an authorized representative of the government takes ownership of supplies delivered under a contract or approves specific services performed under a contract. Acceptance acknowledges that your company's supplies or services conform with all quality or quantity requirements of the contract. Think of acceptance as the formal, official "thumbs up."

You must distinguish acceptance from *delivery* or *performance*. Just because your company mailed products to the federal agency does not mean they were accepted. Just because a federal employee signed for the mailed products does not mean they were accepted. Just because you performed the services does not mean they were accepted. You need to read your contract carefully to determine what constitutes acceptance.

In summary: Delivery is not (necessarily) acceptance. Performance is not (necessarily) acceptance. Acceptance is the official act of the government verifying that whatever your company provided or performed met all requirements of the contract.

Who can provide official acceptance on behalf of the government?

Usually, the contracting officer or some other federal employee will provide acceptance.

What is conditional acceptance?

Conditional acceptance means your company's delivery or performance was "close, but no cigar." Your company needs to fix, cure, correct, supplement, or change something to achieve complete acceptance. Full acceptance is *conditioned* upon your company making the changes.

What is inspection?

Inspection is the process whereby the government examines your supplies or services to determine if they conform to the details of the contract. Before accepting your delivery, the government must verify that you satisfied the standards of the contract.

Who can perform inspection on behalf of the government?

Usually, a federal employee like the contracting officer will perform inspection. Sometimes the contracting officer or contract will designate others to perform inspection. In many contracts, inspection (and testing) is the responsibility of the contractor itself, not the government. You need to carefully read the clauses in your contract related to delivery, inspection, and acceptance.

What are the delivery, inspection, and acceptance terms of my government contract?

I cannot answer this question without reading your government contract. There are several different clauses that change the delivery, inspection, and acceptance terms depending on a wide variety of factors. Government contracts have flexibility to select or alter delivery, inspection, and acceptance terms to adapt to different circumstances.

How should my company mitigate the risk of failing the delivery, inspection, or acceptance stages of government contracting?

Understand that each of your government contracts may have different terms and conditions for delivery, inspection, and acceptance. You need to analyze all clauses or conditions in your contracts related to delivery, inspection, or acceptance carefully. If you cannot handle this task, hire an expert. You can email me at **Christoph@ChristophLLC.com.**

FAR Part 47, Transportation

FAR Part 47 provides transportation policy for government contracting.

What is a carrier?

A *carrier* provides transport services. For example, a company that offers to ship your luggage across the ocean is providing carrier services. The carrier is sometimes called a commercial carrier.

What is common carrier?

A *common carrier* offers and provides transport services to the general public. Anyone can purchase transport services from a common carrier.

What is a contract carrier?

A *contract carrier* provides transport services by individual contracts with one or more clients. Contract carriers are more exclusive than common carriers. Instead of offering transport services to the general public, contract carriers operate on a contract-by-contract basis, perhaps for a limited, continuous set of clients. For example, a contract carrier may contract with a large corporation to move employee household items and office equipment. This contract carrier makes enough money from the single client (the large corporation), so this contract carrier has no need to offer common carrier services to the general public.

Who is the shipper?

The *shipper* asks the carrier to transport items. The carrier transports the items for the shipper. The shipper requests and pays. The carrier makes sure the items arrive where the shipper specifies.

What is a bill of lading?

A *bill of lading* is a document used in transport services. The carrier provides a copy of the bill of lading to the shipper. The bill of lading is a receipt of the items to be transported by the carrier. When passing through checkpoints or customs clearance, the carrier can present the bill of lading to show title to the items, a list of all the items in transport, or as proof of a contract to transport the items.

What is the difference between a commercial bill of lading and a government bill of lading?

A *commercial bill of lading* or *CBL* is prepared for use in the private sector and is not created by a government official. A government bill of lading or GBL is prepared and authorized by a government official.

What is the government's policy for using and accepting a commercial versus government bill of lading?

For domestic shipments within the contiguous United States, the contracting officer is supposed to allow the use of *commercial bills of lading* or *CBL*. The contracting officer may authorize government bills of lading for international shipments or noncontiguous domestic shipments (or in other situations where appropriate). "Contiguous" refers to American states that are connected and share a border. In other words, Alaska and Hawaii are not part of the contiguous United States because they are separated by foreign territory or oceans. Alaska and Hawaii share no borders with any other American state.

What is the preferred method of transporting supplies for the government?

The government's preference is to use commercial carriers, including both common carriers and contract carriers. Generally, the government will use its own vehicles for transport only if it is economical in comparison.

FAR Part 48, Value Engineering

FAR Part 48 explains how your company may suggest contractual efficiencies through the value engineering process.

What is value engineering?

Value engineering is the process whereby the contractor suggests changes to the contract or statement of work that may save cost or time. By proposing a different way of performing the work, the contractor reduces acquisition, operation, or support costs — or finishes the work faster. The government encourages value engineering because the contractor often has a better understanding of the best way forward, so why not listen to what they have to say?

Why would the contractor propose a change that results in less revenue?

The government encourages value engineering by allowing the contractor to share in the cost savings. If the contractor saves the taxpayer money, the contractor gets to keep some of the money saved — a classic "win-win" situation.

How does the contractor propose a value engineering idea?

The contractor submits to the contracting officer a *value engineering change proposal (VECP)*. The value engineering change proposal outlines the required changes to the contract or statement of work, as well as the proposed cost or time savings.

Who has the authority to accept or reject a value engineering change proposal?

The contracting officer will formally accept or reject each value engineering change proposal. Remember, any changes to the contract can be authorized only by the contracting officer. Of course, the contracting officer will probably rely on the analysis and recommendations of a team of government engineers and project managers.

What are the two approaches to value engineering?

The two approaches are *incentive-based value engineering* and *mandatory value engineering*.

What is the difference between incentive-based and mandatory value engineering?

The incentive-based approach is completely voluntary. Your company uses its own resources to develop and propose a value engineering change proposal. Your government contract will specify exactly what percentage of the cost savings your company gets to keep as a reward. The contract will also explain what development and implementation costs are allowable (and therefore reimbursable as payments) during the value engineering process.

The mandatory approach is a requirement of your contract. Using the mandatory approach, your contract will have a line item, deliverable, or clause that requires your company to perform value engineering. The percentage of the cost savings your company receives under the mandatory approach will be less than the percentage received under the incentive-based approach.

No matter what type of value engineering your contract contemplates, your company will not share in any cost savings unless the value engineering cost proposal is accepted and approved by the contracting officer. Therefore, the government has the final decision on any value engineering changes to your contract.

FAR Part 49, Termination of Contracts

FAR Part 49 explores the scariest clause in all of government contracting, and explains the difference between termination for default (or cause) and termination for convenience.

What is a termination clause?

Termination clause doesn't sound very appealing, does it? Death, destruction, ending, finality, time-traveling cybernetic organisms with Austrian accents!

You may be familiar with termination clauses in your apartment lease or cell phone contract. When you want to move early or switch cell phone providers, you read your termination clauses to determine your rights and how to proceed.

How does a termination clause work in government contracting?

In government contracting, the *Termination clauses* allow the government to abruptly fire or terminate your company. You need to understand the three types of Termination clauses: *convenience*, *default*, and *cause*.

What is the scariest clause in all of government contracting?

The scariest clause in all of government contracting is *Termination for Convenience of the Government.* This clause allows the government to abruptly fire or terminate your company without paying the rest of the money from the remaining contract. To put this in perspective, let's contrast it with private sector contracts.

You sign a contract with Donald Trump for $500 million worth of supplies across 5 years, $100 million per year. Your company provides the supplies, Donald Trump provides the $500 million. At the end of the first year, Donald Trump delivers his famous line, "You're fired!" There is no reason for the termination. It occurs simply for the convenience of The Donald.

In private sector contract law, you are entitled now to sue Donald Trump for at least some of the remaining money on the contract. You spent millions of dollars preparing for this 5-year contract. You hired hundreds of professionals. By breaking the deal and violating the contract, The Donald harmed your company or deprived it of future revenue. You can sue The Donald for this future revenue — it's called *expectation damages*. Expectation damages can be thought of as the dollars you expected to receive if The Donald had carried out the terms of the contract rightfully to its conclusion.

Contrast this private sector example with the frightening realm of government contracting. Instead of The Donald, you sign a government contract with the Department of Justice for $500 million worth of services over 5 years, $100 million per year. At the end of the first year, the Department of Justice contracting officer writes you an email that states: "You are hereby terminated for the convenience of the government." Guess what? You cannot sue the government or Department of Justice for the future revenue you lost. You can try, but you will lose. You are not entitled to the *expectation damages* of the broken deal.

Now you see the reasoning behind why the *Termination for Convenience of the Government* is the scariest clause in government contracting. Although you can get paid for a few things after your company is terminated for convenience, you are not entitled to *expectation damages*. Aside from some minor costs your company incurred to wind down the contract, the government walks away with zero liability. This extraordinary power of the government can bankrupt your company.

Terminations for convenience are a risk that almost every government contractor assumes, whether knowingly or in ignorance. You must price in the risk of these terminations for your long-term business plans. Every day the sun rises is another day the government can terminate your entire contract and not pay your company for breaking the deal. Technically, the "deal" or contract says the government can do this and your company agrees!

If my prime contract contains the Termination for Convenience clause, should I include something similar in any subcontracts?

Yes. If your prime contract with the government has the *Termination for Convenience clause*, you need to flow down a version of this clause to your subcontractors. If you do not, then the government can terminate your prime contract, but you are still on the hook to pay all your subcontractors. Remember, your subcontractors can sue you for *expectation damages*. You will be left holding the bag when the government terminates your company for convenience.

To avoid this disastrous situation, include a Termination for Convenience clause flow-down in your subcontracts. Stipulate that your company can use the Termination for Convenience clause against the subcontractor if the government uses the Termination for Convenience clause against your company.

What if my company is the subcontractor performing work for a prime contractor?

If your company is the subcontractor, you should check your subcontract to see if the prime contractor has the right to terminate your company for convenience. If so, you should negotiate to change the subcontract terms to allow the prime contractor to terminate your company *only if* the government terminates the prime contractor.

In other words, do not give any prime contractor the discretion to terminate your subcontract. Allow the prime contractor to terminate your company only to comply with a termination by the government. Include a requirement for the prime contractor to show proof of this termination.

What is the Termination for Cause clause?

When the government procures commercial items (which can be products or services), the government is supposed to use a different clause that does not allow terminations for *default*. Commercial government contracts should include a clause that allows for terminations "for cause."

Terminations for cause in commercial government contracts must be based on some failure of your company. This process differs completely from the scary *Termination for Convenience of the Government clause*. Contract language about termination for cause is nothing to lose sleep over, but actually getting terminated for cause is a nightmare! You can read more about terminations for default to understand why you must avoid terminations for cause or for default.

What is the Termination for Default clause?

In noncommercial government contracts, the contracting officer is supposed to use a version of the Termination clause that allows for termination "for default." Just like the commercial version (*Termination for Cause*), any termination "for default" requires some failure of your company—hence the word "default." Your company has "defaulted" on its responsibility or its ability to fulfill the contract.

If your company is *terminated for default*, this termination may be a death sentence. The termination for default will appear on your company record for years. Other potential government clients will review this information before they decide to award you a contract. At all costs your company must avoid being terminated by default.

If my company is terminated for default, can I fight back in any way?

One way to dodge a termination for default is to convert the bitter pill into a *termination for convenience*. When government contractors litigate or challenge terminations for default, they're sometimes settled, transformed, or ruled by a judge to be a termination for convenience. This change saves the company's reputation in government contracting. That outcome is what your company will want, so try to negotiate a *termination for convenience* rather than a *termination for default*.

What are the warning signs that the government plans to terminate my contract?

The government may send you two warning signs before terminating your company. If you see any correspondence with the words *Cure Notice* or *Show Cause*, you need to go on red alert. Assemble your company's chain of command and get in touch with your expert for government contracting.

What is a Cure Notice?

The *Cure Notice* provides your company a written warning that something is wrong. Your company is doing something or failing to do something that may breach the contract and result in a termination for default. Cure Notice language will read something like this:

> "You are notified that the Government considers your ____ [specify the contractor's failure or failures] a condition that is endangering performance of the contract. Therefore, unless this condition is cured within 10 days after receipt of this notice [or insert any longer time that the Contracting Officer may consider reasonably necessary], the Government may terminate for default under the terms and conditions of the _____ [insert clause title] clause of this contract."

What is a Show Cause Notice?

Show Cause is a more urgent notice that your company may soon be terminated for default. It warns your company to spell out any reasons why the government should not terminate you for default. Usually the Cure Notice comes before the Show Cause Notice, which comes just before your oncoming termination for default. Receiving a Show Cause Notice is like hearing the ominous question, "Any last words?" or "What do you want on your tombstone?" It is your last opportunity for rescue before termination.

FAR Part 50, Extraordinary Contractual Actions and the SAFETY Act

FAR Part 50 provides special powers for the government to create or change contracts to aid the national defense or to fight terrorism.

What is the SAFETY Act?

The full name of the *SAFETY Act* is the *Support Anti-Terrorism by Fostering Effective Technologies Act of 2002.* Congress loves awkward acronyms!

What is the policy goal of the SAFETY Act?

The SAFETY Act provides liability protection for contractors that deliver or perform antiterrorism technology or services. This law shields such contractors from lawsuits and other legal liability, so that such contractors will not be afraid to work with the government on contracts related to preventing or deterring terrorism.

How do I know if my contract is covered by the SAFETY Act protections?

Look for a citation to the SAFETY Act in your contract and look for a FAR clause that starts with "FAR 52.250."

What is an extraordinary contractual action?

To provide special powers for government contracts to support national defense, Congress passed Public Law 85-804 and President Eisenhower signed Executive Order 10789. This law and Executive Order give the President and some federal agencies authorization to enter into, amend, and modify contracts in ways that would be otherwise forbidden or unlawful. These special powers are reserved for emergency situations or to support the national defense. FAR Part 50 implements these special powers, which include the ability to:

Amend contracts without consideration
Correct or mitigate mistakes in contracts
Formalize informal commitments

Can you provide hypothetical examples of the use of these extraordinary powers?

Imagine the United States is currently at war. One of the biggest defense contractors supplies one-half of all American military weapons in this war. One of this defense contractor's contracts has a mistake that will cause the company to go bankrupt. If the company goes bankrupt, the military will not get the weapons to fight the war. So, at the President's direction, the contract is modified without consideration to fix this mistake and "bail out" the contractor.

In another plausible example, no mistake exists in the contract. Instead, by the negotiated terms of the contract, the same defense contractor will sustain heavy financial losses through performance of a vital contract for military weapons. Eventually, the contractor may go bankrupt or become unable to fulfill the contract. Departing from normal contracting laws and regulations due to threats to the national defense, the government can change or adjust the contract or its payment terms to "fix" the situation.

You can see these extraordinary powers allow the government to play favorites and help certain companies to support the national defense. The existence of this policy suggests that President Dwight D. Eisenhower was prophetic when he warned American citizens of the growth of the "military-industrial complex." Some defense contractors and some defense contracts are so important to the national defense that the government reserved the right to suspend contracting laws and regulations to prevent the failure or disruption of these contracts and contractors.

FAR Part 51, Use of Government Sources by Contractors

FAR Part 51 explains how contractors can save time and money by using contracts that would otherwise be available only to the government.

Within FAR Part 51, what does the phrase "government sources" mean?

When you read *government sources* within FAR Part 51, that phrase refers to government contracts that are (usually) available only to the government. If your government contract authorizes you to use government sources, your company may save time and money with this special privilege.

One of the most prominent of these "government sources" is the General Services Administration's Federal Supply Schedule, also called the "GSA Schedule," "GSA Schedule contracts," "FSS contracts," "Multiple Award Schedule," or "the Schedule." You can read more about these contracts in Part 8, Required Sources of Supplies and Services.

In short, *GSA Schedule contracts* provide bulk-pricing discounts for any federal agency that places orders. GSA Schedule contracts offer both supplies and services, all with prenegotiated terms and conditions, including price ceilings (maximum prices that can be negotiated even lower).

Why should my company care about using government sources, like GSA Schedule contracts?

Because you can save money and make your government client happy. Your company—if contractually authorized by a clause prescribed by FAR Part 51—may be able to take advantage of the great deals the government negotiated.

Why would the government let my company use its government sources?

If your company saves time and money in performance of the government contract, your company can pass those savings on to the government client. We have a classic "win-win" situation! If the government is paying for your company's costs in performing the government contract, why *wouldn't* the government client want your company to minimize costs? Your company is happy, the government client is happy, the American taxpayer is happy.

I noticed how FAR Part 51 also mentions something called the "Interagency Fleet Management System Vehicles." What does that mean?

The *Interagency Fleet Management System (IFMS)* is administered by the General Services Administration (GSA) and provides vehicles for official government usage. So, when you read "IFMS," consider it another "government source" that focuses on vehicles. GSA maintains a worldwide fleet of vehicles and vehicle-related products or services, such as fuel, lubricants, inspections, maintenance, repair, and storage. If your government contract contains the IFMS clause prescribed by FAR Part 51, your company can use the IFMS and get great deals otherwise available only for the government.

FAR Part 52, Solicitation Provisions and Contract Clauses

FAR Part 52 contains all the standard contract clauses and solicitation provisions.

Where are all FAR contract clauses located?

FAR Part 52 contains all the standard FAR clauses.

Where are all FAR solicitation provisions located?

FAR Part 52 contains all the standard FAR provisions.

What is the difference between a clause and provision?

Clauses go in the *contract*. Provisions go in the *solicitation*. Therefore, we call them *contract clauses* and *solicitation provisions*. There may be some overlap, such as when a contract clause is found in both the solicitation and resulting contract, but that overlap is to give every potential contractor notice that the clause will apply. If you see the contract clause in the solicitation, that indicates any resulting contract will also include the clause.

Is there a pattern to the numbering of all FAR clauses?

Yes, a simple pattern applies to all FAR clauses, telling you the origin and purpose of each FAR clause.

Why does every FAR clause start with the number 52?

Every FAR clause starts with 52 because all FAR clauses are found in FAR Part 52.

What do the numbers after 52 signify?

After the number 52, every FAR clause has a period or dot, then three numbers, then a dash, then more numbers. Pay attention to the first three numbers after the period.

Of those three numbers, the first will be the number two. That first detail is not important. But the second and third numbers tell you something important about the FAR clause.

What is the secret code of all FAR clause numbers?

If the FAR clause starts with 52.219, that clause derives from FAR Part 19, Small Business Programs. Ignore the 52 and ignore the number two after the period. You are left with 19, which tells you that FAR clause comes from FAR Part 19. Another example is a FAR clause that starts with 52.249. Any FAR clause that starts with 52.249 derives from FAR Part 49, Termination of Contracts.

Why should I care about the FAR Part that corresponds to the FAR clause?

Each FAR clause has specific directions to the contracting officer about when to insert the clause. This detail helps you understand the purpose of the FAR clause and gives you negotiating leverage if you want to remove it before signing the contract.

What is a prescription clause?

Every FAR clause has a *prescription clause* in the beginning of the text of the clause. The prescription clause tells the contracting officer to insert the clause into contracts under certain circumstances. For example, insert the clause into any contracts for construction greater than $5 million, or insert the clause into any contracts performed overseas.

If the circumstances of your government contract do not match the prescription clause for a FAR clause currently in your contract, try to get the contracting officer to remove the FAR clause. If you find this discrepancy before signing the contract, ask to remove the clause before signature.

Even if you are performing a contract that you signed years ago, you might be able to persuade the contracting officer to remove an inappropriate clause. Your most powerful method of persuasion is to reference the prescription clause and demonstrate that your contract is not applicable.

What does "incorporate by reference" mean?

Incorporate by reference means your contract lists the number and title of the FAR clause, but not the full text of the clause. Your contract may include more than one hundred FAR clauses. The full text of so many FAR clauses will take up valuable space in the contract. Instead of including the full text, the contracting officer can "incorporate by reference" some of the FAR clauses.

For example, you may see a single line in your contract that states:

"FAR 52.243-1 Changes, Fixed-Price (Aug 1987)"

Even though the contracting officer did not include the full text of FAR 52.243-1, you are responsible for following the full text of FAR 52.243-1. Incorporating a clause by reference saves space and makes the contract easier to read. However, you need to be careful because you remain responsible for the entirety of whatever FAR clause is incorporated by reference.

What does "incorporate by full text" mean?

Incorporate by full text means the contracting officer includes the complete text of the FAR clause in your contract. You will see the number and title of the FAR clause as well as a paragraph or more underneath, consisting of the full text of the clause.

What does "ALT" or "alternate" signify in the title of a FAR clause?

Some FAR clauses have alternate versions to use for different circumstances, although the substance or topic of each clause remains the same. For example, there are several alternates for the Changes clause for cost-reimbursement contracts. The alternate versions apply depending on whether the contract is for services, supplies, or construction. Yet all versions or alternates are Changes clauses which apply to the cost-reimbursement contracts.

What does the date after the FAR clause mean?

You may notice the FAR clauses in your contract have a date, usually within parentheses, after the number and title. Just as the rest of the FAR is updated constantly, FAR clauses are also frequently updated. Therefore, the date after the FAR clause refers to the last update to that FAR clause. The date is referred to as the "version" of the FAR clause to distinguish it from earlier or later revisions of the same FAR clause.

What if my FAR clause does not include a date after the number and title?

The contracting officer should always include a date after the number and title, so this situation indicates a mistake or oversight. In this case, you should be responsible for performing the latest version of that FAR clause in existence as of the date you signed the contract. Finding out which version applies may require intense research into previous or archived editions of the FAR.

When a FAR clause referenced in my contract is updated and replaced by a newer version, but my contract did not change, do my responsibilities under the contract change?

No, not if your contract has not changed, and this point is important for you to remember. You negotiated a deal when you signed the government contract. The bargain included the FAR clauses in the contract as of the date you signed the contract. You cannot be responsible for constantly changing clauses. Your company is responsible for the versions of the FAR clauses in the contract as indicated by their dates. In the absence of specified dates, you are responsible for the latest versions of the FAR clauses in effect at the time you signed the contract.

What if the contracting officer wants to update one or more FAR clauses in my contract to newer versions?

Changing a FAR clause changes your responsibilities under the contract. Changing your responsibilities under the contract may cause your company to spend more time or money. Therefore, changing any FAR clause may entitle your company to an *equitable adjustment*. In plain English, an "equitable adjustment" means your company gets more money, a schedule extension, or some other type of contractual relief.

Can the contracting officer update my FAR clauses when exercising the option?

Yes, but by changing the FAR clauses, the government loses its right to exercise the option unilaterally (without your permission). Your company agreed to perform the option period when it signed the contract, but your company did not agree to the updates to the FAR clause. The contracting officer must separate these modifications to retain the right to unilaterally exercise your option.

While the contracting officer can combine the option exercise with other changes, this combination means your company may be entitled to an "equitable adjustment," meaning money, schedule extensions, or other contractual relief.

Why should I investigate further if the contracting officer requests my signature when exercising an option?

Let's say your contracting officer sends your company a modification to exercise the next option period and requires your signature. This seems like welcome news. Your company receives new work and an extension of the period of performance. Your company gets 365 more days of revenue from this contract.

Be careful if the government requests your signature. Technically, there is no need for your company to countersign the option exercise. The government has the right to exercise the option unilaterally. That pattern is how options work. The government does not need your permission to exercise the option under standard FAR clauses, so the government may request your signature for you to accept other changes in the contract, such as updates to FAR clauses.

If your company does not need to countersign an option exercise modification, the government has no reason to ask for your signature (other than an innocent reason: to ensure your company realizes the option was exercised). This request for signature could mean your company is signing away its rights on several other issues.

Be careful. Make sure to read the details of the modification. The government might not tell you how the modification to exercise the option has some other important changes. Send a copy of the modification to your designated government contracting expert before you sign it. Make sure you review every modification, especially those described as "no big deal."

What is a self-deleting clause?

There is no such thing as a self-deleting clause. Be very careful with any "professionals" who talk about self-deleting clauses.

The erroneous theory behind this canard is that if any clause is inappropriate for the contract, it is somehow "self-deleting" automatically. Therefore, you might not need to worry about the clause being written into the contract you have read and signed. This is an absurd idea.

Do any clauses automatically disappear, like a magician's trick?

No, clauses do not automatically disappear. Are these clauses written with disappearing ink from a child's magic store? No. Does the page of the contract that contains the clause automatically self-destruct after 24 hours, like some James Bond movie? No. The clause remains in your contract for one and all to read.

After litigation, some clauses might be found by a judge to be unenforceable, illegal, or otherwise rendered inoperative. But to rely on the nonexistent legal principle of "self-deleting" clauses during negotiations is the unmistakable mark of an amateur.

What should I do if I see a clause that does not belong in my contract?

If you see a clause that does not belong in your contract, negotiate to delete that clause. Do not accept an explanation of how the clause self-deletes. If the clause is supposedly self-deleting anyway, why should your negotiation partner care if you delete it? Negotiate to delete the clause.

How many FAR clauses exist?

The sheer number of Federal Acquisition Regulation (FAR) clauses is easily overwhelming. Don't ask me to count them because their numbers just keep rising. Luckily for you, some clauses are easily recognized as more important than others. These critical clauses should be your priority when you review your government contract. If one of the following clauses is in your government contract, take the time to read the complete clause or hire a professional to walk you through it.

Why are clauses related to payment so important?

Your company needs to be paid on time in full. Cash flow is the lifeblood of business. Pay special attention to your payment clauses. Your contract with the government will not have much flexibility regarding payment clauses, but you should take special note of the payment terms. Your payment terms from the government should necessarily define the payment terms you negotiate with your subcontractors. You want to avoid the responsibility of paying subcontractors before your own company gets paid.

When you negotiate a contract or subcontract with another company, you have the greatest amount of flexibility in payment terms. Be extremely careful about the details of payment clauses.

What is a "pay when paid" term, condition, or clause?

Never sign a contract that says something like "We will pay you when we get paid." This can be a disaster for your company. As a subcontractor, you can be several payment transactions separated from the government, who begins the cycle by paying the prime contractor first. If the government is 90 days late, the prime contractor will not pay your company for at least 90 days. Delays can get much worse if your company is a lower tier subcontractor, buried beneath tiers of other subcontractors waiting to get paid. You must avoid *pay when paid* contract terms.

Explain to your negotiation partner that the contract is between your two companies. If the government or any other company breaks its promises or fails to pay, that should not affect the contractual relationship between your two companies. Do not let your negotiation partner mix your company's interests with the potential failures of other parties. Do not let other people's problems become your problem. Keep the negotiation about payment terms between your company and the negotiation partner.

What is the Changes clause?

Several versions of the *Changes clause* allow the government to change the contract unilaterally, within certain limits. These limits depend on which version of the Changes clause exists in your contract. Contracting officers use different versions of the Changes clause based upon such factors as whether your contract is fixed price or cost reimbursement or whether your company provides supplies or services.

The biggest wildcard for any government contract is the Changes clause. Most contracts establish the rights and responsibilities of the parties while providing a specific task to perform or product to deliver. Sometimes the contract includes a Statement of Work (SOW) or specifications to follow. Most contracts allow your company to foresee exactly what it will do to fulfill the contract. The Changes clause turns that concept on its head.

At any time, the government contracting officer can send you a modification to the contract pursuant to the Changes clause. This message will not be a negotiation. Your company cannot decline. Instead, by signing the original contract including the Changes clause, your company has already agreed to any such unilateral changes! If the Changes clause sounds unfair to you as the contractor, you have paid attention to my advice.

Never forget that the Changes clause does not give authority to the government to make unlimited changes. These changes must be exactly the same changes listed in your version of the Changes clause. Most versions of the Changes clause allow unilateral changes to such matters as product specifications, services to be delivered, and place of performance or delivery.

Most importantly of all, remember that the Changes clause does not require your company to work for free. Changes cost money and the government is required to compensate your company. When the contracting officer sends your company a unilateral modification pursuant to the Changes clause, your first thought should be to calculate the cost of compliance. Then you need to get paid by submitting a request for equitable adjustment (REA) or claim under the Contract Disputes Act. For more information, read Part 33, Protests, Disputes, and Appeals.

What are the Termination clauses?

Termination clause doesn't sound very appealing, does it? Death, destruction, ending, finality, time-traveling cybernetic organisms with Austrian accents!

Just like it seems, the Termination clauses allow the government to abruptly fire or terminate your company. You need to understand the three types of Termination clauses: convenience, default, and cause. Read more about the Termination clauses in Part 49, Termination of Contracts.

What is so important about delivery, inspection, and acceptance clauses?

Strictly adhering to clauses related to delivery, inspection, and acceptance will determine whether your company succeeds or spirals into a costly failure. Scan your contract for anything related to delivery, inspection, and acceptance (or refusal). You need to know when, where, and how to deliver the supplies or services your contract requires. Before you sign the contract, make sure you understand precisely how you must deliver. This analysis is not limited to supplies.

If your government contract is for services, you also need to know where and when to perform the services. Do you need access to a military base or government-owned building? Do your employees need security clearances? Will your employees need to follow a schedule set by the government rather than your company's management? Will your company be paid for time during federal holidays, when the government is closed and when workers are unoccupied?

For you to be paid, first your company must deliver. Then the government inspects and accepts. Keep in mind that inspection and acceptance is not always performed by the same person or even the same office. You need to have some idea of how the government will inspect and accept whatever your company provides under the contract. What factors lead to a success or failure during inspection? Will everything be inspected or a test sample only? How much time can the government take during inspection? How long can the government wait before pronouncing acceptance or rejection of the delivery?

Such questions can make or break a government contract. Details of delivery, inspection, and acceptance are vital. Do not be afraid to ask questions about these topics. Carefully read and analyze any section of the contract that deals with delivery, inspection, or acceptance.

What are the Limitations on Subcontracting clauses?

The *Limitations on Subcontracting clauses* strictly control how much and to whom you can subcontract work under your prime contract with the government. For more information, read Part 19, Small Business Programs.

What is so important about clauses about submission of certified cost or pricing data?

Read about your company's requirements to submit *certified cost or pricing data* (and the exceptions!) in Part 15, Contracting by Negotiation.

Can you provide a strategic analysis and executive summary of the important clauses, terms, and conditions in all my government contracts?

Maybe. Ask for my help by sending an email to **Christoph@ChristophLLC.com**.

Do you offer online training about these topics?

Yes! Complete my online courses available at **Courses.ChristophLLC.com**.

FAR Part 53, Forms

FAR Part 53 contains guidance for standard forms used in government contracting.

Where can I find official forms?

The General Services Administration (GSA) maintains an online database of forms. The GSA website is **www.gsa.gov**.

What is the Standard Form (SF) 1402?

SF 1402, *Certificate of Appointment*, is the form for a contracting officer warrant to sign, administer, modify, and terminate contracts. The SF 1402 is referred to as the contracting officer's "warrant." You can request a copy of the warrant of your contracting officer to verify the ability to sign your company's contracts. Learn more about contracting officer warrants in Introductory Chapter 1.

What is SF 1449?

SF 1449, *Solicitation/Contract/Order for Commercial Items*, is the preferred form for solicitations or purchase orders for commercial products or commercial services. You may encounter the SF 1449 during simplified acquisition procedures of FAR Part 13, or when the government combines the commercial procedures of FAR Part 12 with other contract competition methods.

What is SF 18?

SF 18, *Request for Quotations*, is the form for requesting price quotations.

What is SF 30?

SF 30, *Amendment of Solicitation/Modification of Contract*, is the form for amending the solicitation or modifying your government contract. You can expect to see several modifications using the SF 30 during your contracting career.

What is SF 26?

SF 26, *Award/Contract*, is the form to sign a new contract with your company. Hopefully, you will become familiar with the SF 26 as your company wins more contracts.

What is the DD 254 form?

You will become familiar with the DD 254 if you perform contracts with security classification requirements. *Department of Defense (DD) Form 254* conveys the security requirements for contractors who require access to classified information. You may have heard of various classification levels, such as "Secret" or "Top Secret."

Conclusion: Are You a Professional?

Professionalism is about action. Professionalism is not status, title, or certification. Your actions and behavior define you as a professional. A professional is intellectually curious about his field of expertise. You need to read about other professionals and pay attention to what they do and say. Ideally, once you get to the point where you can add something substantive on your own, you should publish an article to spread the knowledge. Even better, train your colleagues on a topic of your choice.

I challenge you to think about something. Do you consider yourself a professional? Why? What makes you a professional? What if someone denied that you are a professional? If you had to prove it, what evidence will you use to show you are a professional? How will you defend yourself? What will you say?

I believe that actions define the professional, so I know what I will say. As an expert witness, consultant, author, and instructor, my actions are those of a professional. I strive to continually learn more about government contracting. I share my knowledge and collaborate with fellow professionals. I contribute to the profession by advancing the body of knowledge through published articles, teaching, commentary in the press, and advice in this book. I consider my actions to be those of a professional in the field of government contracting.

I don't have any customers. I have clients. When you have a client, you act as a subject matter expert, advancing the interests of that client while steering them away from potential problems and unnecessary risk. That's what a government contracting professional should be doing. Is that what you're doing?

What do you want? Do you want to be an administrator who mindlessly processes things? Would you rather be a professional who learns the reasoning behind the rules and processes? Do you want customers or clients? Do you want to be a clerk or a professional?

Decide who you are, right now. Stick to it like the integrity of your career depends upon it, because it does. Maybe one day you'll find yourself in a job where you know you have no potential for advancement or development. Maybe someone will tell you to do something you know is wrong or illegal. When something like this happens, remember this discussion. Go look in the mirror. Make an important decision. *Are you a professional?* Only you will know the answer. You will be reminded of your choice every time you look in the mirror.

Thank you for reading my book! Stay in touch. Email me at **Christoph@ChristophLLC.com** and complete my online courses at **Courses.ChristophLLC.com**.

Index

Acceptance, 253
Acquisition planning, 57
Administrative change, 235
Administrative contracting officer (ACO), 233
Administrative modification, 235
Advance payment bond, 181
Advance payments, 194
Agency ethics official, 37
Agency protests, 203
Agency supplements, 16
Air Force FAR Supplement (AFFARS), 16
Allocable, 192
Allowability, 191
Ambiguity, 32
Annual bid bond, 181
Annual performance bond, 182
Appropriated money, 44
Approved purchasing system, 242
Architect-engineer (A-E) services, 217
Automatic stay, 206
Award fees, 133
Base period, 143
Bid, 179
Bid bond, 181
Bid guarantee, 179
Bilateral modification, 235
Bill of lading, 258
Bond, 180
Brand name only, 82
Brand name or equal, 82
Broad Agency Announcements (BAA), 211
Brooks Act, 218
Bundling, 58
Carrier, 257
Cash flow, 193
Ceiling prices, 68
Change order, 236
Changes clause, 198,

Claim, 197
Code of Business Ethics and Conduct, 34
Code of Federal Regulations (CFR), 22
Commercial bill of lading (CBL), 258
Commercial items, 81
Common carrier, 257
Competition in Contracting Act (CICA), 99
Conditional acceptance, 254
Consolidation, 58
Constructive change, 237
Contingency operation, 149
Contract action, 44
Contract action report, 44
Contract carrier, 257
Contract financing, 193
Contract Line Item Numbers (CLINs), 143
Contracting officers, 5
Contracting officer's representative (COR), 6
Contractor Acquired Property (CAP), 251
Contractor bid or proposal information, 37
Contractor Performance Assessment Reporting System (CPARS), 110
Contractor Purchasing System Review (CPSR), 243
Cooperative agreements, 214
Cost Accounting Standards (CAS), 187
Cost Accounting Standards Board (CASB), 187
Cost or pricing data, 121
Cost overrun, 129
Cost plus fixed fee (CPFF), 131
Cost-reimbursement, 129
Cure Notice, 265
Davis-Bacon Act (DBA), 166
Debriefing, 117

Defense Contract Audit Agency (DCAA), 233
Defense Contract Management Agency (DCMA), 233
Defense FAR Supplement (DFARS), 16
Delegation, 24
Delivery order (DO), 64
Department of Defense (DD) Form 254, 284
Determination and findings (D&F), 29
Deviation, 26
Discovery, 205
Doctrine of constructive changes, 237
Economically disadvantaged, women-owned small businesses (EDWOSB), 155
Equitable adjustment, 237
Estimated cost ceiling, 132
Evaluation factor, 107
Exercise an option, 144
Expectation damages, 262
Experience, 111
Fair opportunity, 140
Federal Awardee Performance and Integrity Information System (FAPIIS), 73
Federal Procurement Data System (FPDS), 43
Federal Register, 15
Federal Supply Schedule (FSS) contracts, 64
Final Decision, 200
Firm fixed price (FFP), 134
Fixed-price contract, 129
Freedom of Information Act (FOIA), 171
Full and open competition, 51
Full and open competition after exclusion of sources, 52
Fully loaded labor rate, 136
Funding availability, 213
General liability insurance, 183

Government Accountability Office (GAO) bid protest, 202
Government Furnished Property (GFP), 251
Government property, 251
Government sources, 269
Governmentwide point of entry (GPE), 48
Grants, 214
GSA Advantage, 65
GSA CALC Tool, 65
GSA E-Buy, 66
GSA E-Library, 65
GSA Schedule contracts, 269
Historically underutilized business zone small businesses (HUBZone), 155
Importance to agency programs, 214
Incentive-based value engineering, 260
Incentive fees, 133
Incorporate by full text, 273
Incorporate by reference, 273
Indefinite-delivery, definite-quantity contracts, 141
Indefinite-delivery, indefinite-quantity (IDIQ) contracts, 63
Indian Incentive Program, 175
Industrial mobilization, 55
Inherently governmental function, 59
Inspection, 254
Interagency Fleet Management System (IFMS), 270
International agreement, 55
Invitation for Bids (IFB), 99
Justification and Approval (J&A), 54
Labor-hour contracts, 135
Life-cycle cost, 57
Limitation of Cost, 132
Limitation of Funds, 132
Limitations on Pass-Through Charges clause, 156
Limitations on Subcontracting clauses, 156

Lowest price, technically acceptable (LPTA), 106
Major Defense Acquisition Program (MDAP), 209
Mandatory value engineering, 260
Market research, 75
Multiple Award Schedule (MAS) contracts, 64
National Defense Authorization Act (NDAA), 27
National security, 55
Nonresponsive, 100
North American Industry Classification System (NAICS) codes, 152
Only one source, 55
Option periods, 143
Oral presentation, 116
Ordering activity, 64
Other competitive procedures, 53
Other than certified cost or pricing data, 123
Other than full and open competition, 54
Other Transactions, 215
Past performance, 108
Past performance questionnaires (PPQs), 110
Patent infringement bond, 182
Pay when paid, 195
Payment bond, 182
Peer or scientific review, 213
Performance-based acquisition, 219
Performance-based payments, 194
Performance bond, 182
Performance Work Statement (PWS), 219
Personal services, 221
Precedent, 11
Prescription clause, 272
Price premium, 104
Prime contractor, 245
Privity of contract, 246

Procurement Contracting Officer (PCO), 244
Procurement Instrument Identifier (PIID), 41
Procurement Integrity Act, 38
Professional liability insurance, 183
Progress payments, 194
Prompt Payment Act, 194
Protest, 197
Program managers, 7
Public interest, 55
Qualifications-based selection, 218
Quality Assurance Surveillance Plan (QASP), 220
Ratification, 28
Reasonable, 192
Research and development contracting, 211
Responsibility, 101
Responsibility determination, 71
Responsive, 100
Responsiveness, 101
Request for equitable adjustment (REA), 198
Request for Proposals (RFP), 51
Requests for Information (RFI), 77
Requirements contract, 141
Requiring activity, 64
Robert T. Stafford Disaster Relief and Emergency Assistance Act, 176
SAFETY Act, 267
Sealed bids, 99
Service Contract Act (SCA), 165
Service-disabled, veteran-owned small businesses (SDVOSB), 155
Shipper, 257
Show Cause, 266
Small business, 152
Small business set-aside, 151
Small disadvantaged businesses (SDB), 156
Sole-source government contract, 83
Solicitation provisions, 271
Source selection authority (SSA), 105

Source selection decision document, 105
Sources sought notice (SSN), 77
Simplified acquisition threshold (SAT), 92
Standard Form 1402 (SF 1402) Certificate of Appointment, 283
Standard Form 1449 (SF 1449) Solicitation/Contract/Order for Commercial Items, 283
Standard Form 18 (SF 18) Request for Quotations, 283
Standard Form 30 (SF 30) Amendment of Solicitation/Modification of Contract, 283
Statute, 55
Subcontract, 245
Subcontractor, 245
Supplemental agreement, 235
Surety company, 181
System for Award Management (SAM), 48
Task order (TO), 64
Technical, 214
Technical approach, 108
Terminated for default, 264
Termination clause, 261
Termination for cause, 264
Termination for Convenience clause, 263
Termination for convenience of the government, 261
Termination for default, 264
Time and materials contract, 135
Tradeoff, 103
Truth in Negotiations Act (TINA), 120
Two-step sealed bidding, 101
Unauthorized commitment, 28
Under similar circumstances, 69
Unilateral modification, 235
Unilateral right, 144
Urgency, 55
Value engineering, 259
Value engineering change proposal (VECP), 259
Veteran-owned small businesses (VOSB), 155
Wage determination, 166
Walsh-Healey Public Contracts Act (PCA), 167
Warrant, 5
Women-owned small business (WOSB) set-aside, 52
Women-owned small businesses (WOSB), 155
Workers' compensation insurance, 183
Wrap rate, 137
8(a) business development program, 156

Made in United States
North Haven, CT
02 February 2023